I0055909

PRAISE FOR

Take Ownership of What You Own

"David's book has filled a major gap in the literature dealing with family Trusts – fully illuminating and encompassing the whole question of a Trust as owner. Further, he has elucidated and offered positive solutions to a critical issue of family Trusts: how can a beneficiary healthily integrate a Trust into his or her life? His notion of a "Self Governing Beneficiary" alone will make his book a classic in the field of wealth and well-being. I strongly recommend this book."

—**JAMES (JAY) E. HUGHES, JR.**, *author of Family Wealth: Keeping it in the Family and Family: The Compact Among Generations; co-author of Family Trusts*

"David has taken such a thoughtful approach to helping members of a family enterprise understand their roles as owners, and integrate those roles with who they are and who they want to be – giving each family member permission to individuate and differentiate from their predecessors. Building on the idea that each generation is, in some ways, the first generation, he invites future family leaders and owners not to fear their ownership. Any beneficiary, owner, or child of a prior generation of entrepreneurs who feels stuck, ashamed, unworthy, or untrusted will feel empowered by David's words."

—**JOSH KANTER**, *Founder of leafplanner and President of Chicago Financial*

"'Keep the people at the center, and lose no one.' With Meriwether Lewis as his guide, David Burleigh takes us on a journey into the wilderness of family trusts. With wisdom, insight, and humanity, Burleigh acknowledges the real challenges of being a trust beneficiary, while encouraging us to discover greater purpose, meaning, and ultimately, self-governance."

—**AMELIA RENKERT-THOMAS,** *author of Engaged Ownership: A Guide for Owners of Family Businesses and Professor at University of North Carolina, Chapel Hill*

"David Burleigh has written a unique and very much needed book dealing with ownership and succession of that ownership. He comes from a place of considerable experience, wisdom, and professional expertise. Anyone dealing with succession of an enterprise should find this book to be extremely beneficial. I recommended it highly."

—**RON BLUE,** *Founder of Ronald Blue & Company*

"As former chair of the trusts and estates practice of a large law firm, I find here a terrific guide. David does an excellent job of explaining trusts in simple terms and how a well-designed trust agreement can serve a family over generations. His concept of "shared ownership" among the creator, beneficiaries and future descendants is right on."

—**MARK SWARY,** *Co-Founder of Western Reserve Trust Company*

"All family enterprise owners, including trustees and beneficiaries, should reflect on how well they integrate what they own with who they are. David explains this compelling idea with characteristic clarity and elegance. He reminds us of the importance of a shared purpose for owners and explains the concepts of being a Self-Governing Beneficiary and an Entrepreneurial Steward. Family enterprise owners and their advisers should really read this book."

—**KEN MCCRACKEN,** *Founder of McCracken Family Business Consulting, Edinburgh, Scotland*

"Business - Ownership - Family: these are way more than words. The way David uses his genius and his experience helps readers arrive at a better understanding of both the good and the bad, and brings us along the journey to better. David has been a trusted advisor for me, and I am a better person because of his help."

—**MARY MILLER,** *President of The Dream Engineer and Former Chief Executive Officer of Jancoa, Inc.*

"Our family and business is large and multi-generational, with lineal descendants and in-laws working together, yet with most family shareholders not active in the business. David has worked with us for years and brings peace, calm, and wisdom in helping us realize our shared purpose. His book brings these same qualities."

—**PAUL VERST,** *Chief Executive Officer of Verst Logistics*

"This book reminds me, as someone who tends to lead with my heart, that my co-owners have a perspective unique to them from a lifetime of learning and experiences that I'll never have. The book provides me a sharper framework for making judgments and decisions that honor my co-owners, reflect the history of our family, and use the talents each of us has to take on the future."

—**GREGORY W. OLSON,** *Chief Executive Officer of Urban Sites*

"David's book is the innovative tool for family leaders to refine your thinking on ownership, fulfill fiduciary responsibilities to future generations, and express your own legacy – all while keeping the peace."

—**JAMIE OVERBEY,** *Top 20 Master Chair Worldwide, Vistage International*

"This book does an incredible job of breaking down the basic principles and mechanics of a trust in a way a non-expert can understand. Even more, I found it inspiring to imagine all the possibilities once you open yourself to an ownership mindset."

—**TERESA TANNER,** *Chief Executive Officer of Reserve Squad, LLC; Former Executive Vice President and Chief Administrative Officer of Fifth Third Bank, N.A.*

"Not only does Burleigh de-mystify the tools involved in family ownership, he brilliantly places them in an integrated framework that will keep families productive, purposeful—

and together—across generations."

—**THOMAS "WOODY" TAFT,** *President of Taft Holdings*

"As a former Outward Bound instructor and family office advisor, I am excited to share David's wisdom with the younger members of my own family. Three important lessons I learned: discover your own Unique Ability, learn to lead a unique team, and get out of your comfort zone. This book takes those themes to a new level."

—**ALAN W. PEACOCK,** *Outdoor Leadership Expert and Family Office Advisor, Stormfield, LLC*

TAKE OWNERSHIP OF WHAT YOU OWN

BUILD YOUR CONFIDENCE TO NAVIGATE THE WORLD OF TRUSTS AND FAMILY ENTERPRISE

DAVID W. BURLEIGH

TAKE OWNERSHIP OF WHAT YOU OWN
Build Your Confidence to Navigate the World of Trusts and Family Enterprise
First Edition

ISBN 978-1-962341-49-3 *Hardcover*
978-1-962341-48-6 *Paperback*
978-1-962341-51-6 *Ebook*
978-1-962341-50-9 *Audiobook*

This book is in honor of
Michael P. Jackson, retired Deputy Secretary of
Homeland Security of the United States of America
and a person of total integrity;
and in memory of
Ann Gravel Vanderslice, a fine Southern
writer, a family anchor, and a true friend;
and Father Matthew T. Gamber, S.J., who always
made himself available and helped many people by
performing essential tasks over and over again.

CONTENTS

INTRODUCTION

FACING THE INTEGRITY PROBLEM

"This test is designed to raise your grade."

—KARL HAUCK, SEPTEMBER 1983

This is a book about happiness, family, and money.

We all want happiness. Happiness is satisfying. It may be the most satisfying thing you can experience. I've never met someone who didn't want to be happy. I've met people who went about happiness in a way that did not *make* them happy—but they certainly wanted happiness, just as everyone else wants it.

We also all want a harmonious family, and yet for so many, family is often a source of unease. Maybe you get along with your family; maybe you don't. In either case, your family forms your earliest human relationships, and as a result your family leaves an indelible impact on how you move through the world. Family affects the relationships you have with any number of people—your parents, your siblings, your cousins, your friends, your colleagues at work, people you know in the community. Family affects who you like and who you don't. In thinking about your family now, are you just a little bit on edge? You're not alone.

Now add money to the mix. Money is another thing everyone wants, but almost *no one* wants to combine family and money, because they're quite aware of the fraught nature of such an intersection. Money is a tool—a uniquely powerful tool. You want to be able to control it when you need it. Unfortunately for family harmony, so does everyone else in your family. Sometimes they even want to control it so they *don't* need it. There never seems to be enough money to do everything that needs doing. For good or bad, money makes the relationships you have with your family more complex.

So, how does one smoothly navigate a scenario where all three things—happiness, family, and money—are tied together through ownership?

There are things you own by yourself —your car, for example. Other things you might own with people who aren't in your family—an accounting firm you own with partners outside your family. And then there are things you might own with people who *are* in your family—a house, a long-standing family business, a piece of vacation property, a family farm.

The co-ownership of assets with your family is the focus of this book. We'll spend a lot of time looking at how you co-own things with your family, especially things that are owned in trust. By the time you finish reading this book, you will understand how a trust works—music to the ears of anyone mired in an opaque tangle of trust ownership and administration.

If you're a family owner trying to make sense of this asset that means so much to you, your family, and generations to come—and wondering how to integrate that asset into your life in a way that makes it feel like a boon, not a burden—then I wrote this book for you. With what you'll learn in the chapters to come, you'll be able to take ownership of what you own.

OUR DISCONNECTED, ISOLATED LANDSCAPE

Today's cultural landscape makes dealing with family and money, and trying to attain happiness when it comes to them, especially difficult. We live in a time when many people feel disconnected and isolated, even from their own family. The disconnection makes them worried, and the isolation makes them downright depressed.

If you feel disconnected from people in your family, especially where money is concerned, you're not alone. A money discussion in a family usually involves two or even three generations of people. Often, neither the older generation nor the younger knows how to make the first move. Think about this: well over half of "Baby Boomer" parents (people born from 1946 to 1964) aren't confident their children are well prepared to receive an inheritance.[1] Yet at the same time, upwards of half collectively of Millennial children (people born from 1981 to 1996) and of Gen Z children (people born from 1997 to 2012) aren't confident they know how to handle an inheritance.[2] Neither the older generation nor the younger generation is confident about transferring money within a family. The disconnection between them is pronounced, and it leaves those of all ages across a family without the confidence they need to successfully navigate ownership and integration of what they own.

Compounding the problem is the very serious developing sense of isolation many people feel. According to 2020 United States census data, over one quarter of all households in the United States consist of just one person.[3] About 40% of these individuals are age 65 and older.[4] In this same year, 2020, in response to a major survey, 61% of Americans reported they are lonely.[5]

Meanwhile, at the younger end of the population, nearly 50% of American youth report feeling they can't do anything right, their life is not useful, and they don't enjoy their life.[6] Sui-

1 Al W. King III, "Population Trends and Trust Planning," Trusts & Estates, November 2023.

2 Id., citing Chloe Berger article in Fortune, July 2023, www.fortune.com/2023/07/21/boomers-great-wealth-transfer-millenials-pros-cons/. The figures are 61% of Baby Boomer parents, 21% of Millenial children, and 18% of Gen Z children.

3 See United States Census Bureau article, June 8, 2023, https://www.census.gov/library/stories/2023/06/more-than-a-quarter-all-households-have-one-person.html

4 Id.

5 Michael S. Erwin and Willys Devoll, *Leadership Is Relationship: How to Put People First in the Digital World* (Wiley 2022), p. xvi.

6 "Monitoring the Future," University of Michigan research study by Dr. Jean

cide is now the second leading cause of death among teenagers in the United States.[7]

Perhaps not coincidentally, the average American watches television four times longer each day than they spend socializing and communicating with other people.[8] This is in addition to the time Americans spend viewing screens on phones, desktop computers, and other electronic devices. We binge-watch, we doomscroll, and largely we do it alone.

As for young people in particular, 45% of teenagers report they are tied to the Internet "almost constantly."[9] As a result, for about 16 hours per day, or 112 hours per week, they are not fully present to what is happening around them.[10] Heavy users of social media apps receive from their phones close to one interruption every minute.[11] The current culture's use of technology has led one professor at Massachusetts Institute of Technology

---

Twenge, Ph.D. (analyzing pre-Covid-19 pandemic data), reported in New York Post, June 19, 2023; see Twenge, *Generations: The Real Differences Between Gen Z, Millenials, Gen X, Boomers and Silent—and What They Mean for America's Future* (Atria Books 2023); see also Jonathan Haidt, *The Anxious Generation: How The Great Rewiring of Childhood Is Causing an Epidemic of Mental Illness*, pp. 21-45, 270(Penguin Press 2024).

7 National Alliance on Mental Illness report, Suicide Prevention Month | NAMI: National Alliance on Mental Illness, citing data from Centers for Disease Control National Center for Health Statistics, reported June 2023 (NCHS Data Brief No. 471), Products - Data Briefs - Number 471 - June 2023 (cdc.gov), and 2020 data from National Institutes of Mental Health, Suicide - National Institute of Mental Health (NIMH) (nih.gov).

8 Erwin, *Leadership is Relationship*, p, xvii.

9 Haidt, *The Anxious Generation*, pp. 34, 119.

10 Id., p. 119.

11 Id., p. 120.

to comment, "We are forever elsewhere."[12]

Family members, especially those who co-own things with each other, can't afford to be disconnected and isolated. In this book, I do not claim that money is the solution to our growing disconnection and isolation. Money is a tool, not a way of life. What I do claim is that family co-owners must not allow themselves to become disconnected and isolated. The emotional cost of family members being isolated is obvious. The financial and operational costs, though less obvious, are also a huge drain on family owners.

Family owners need confidence. The purpose of this book is to provide that confidence. My goal is that when you finish reading this book, you feel confident in navigating the world of trusts and family enterprise.

THE INTEGRITY PROBLEM

To get the confidence you need, you will have to confront what I call the Integrity Problem.

Confidence with family and money is challenging because it poses a question of integrity. This doesn't mean that people who own valuable assets—cash in a trust, investment accounts, land, buildings, equipment, vehicles—lack integrity. It doesn't mean they are dishonest. It doesn't mean they are corrupt. It

12 Id., p. 34.

doesn't mean they are bad people, as the news often wants us to believe. Instead, it means someone who is an owner, especially a family owner, faces a special challenge in becoming whole and undivided.

In this book, the Integrity Problem refers to the challenge of integrating two things: what you own, and who you are. It means integrating into your life the things you own and the ownership relationships you have with people in your family. Integrity is the result of integrating, or combining, parts in order to create a whole. Integration is the process. Integrity is the result.

In particular, in this book, integration means integrating into your life things you own in a family trust. Many people view a trust as a piece of machinery that sits outside of the rest of their life. That's not the best way to view or run a family trust. There's a better way, which I will explain. With a trust, and with anything else your family owns, the goal is for you and your family to be as close to whole as you realistically can be.

The Integrity Problem is real. Talking around it, or acting like it doesn't exist, will not help you. The way to address the problem is to tackle it head-on. That's what we will do in this book.

FEELING INTIMIDATED AND BUILDING CONFIDENCE

Here's the truth: many people find the world of trusts and family ownership intimidating. It's a world of technical legal concepts, unintuitive principles, and treacherous emotional terrain. It deals with money, family relationships, control, and freedom—a combination guaranteed to make people nervous. If it were a class, most of the students would fear getting a bad grade.

The good news is that you don't need to feel intimidated. There's a better way to take the class, where you get a grade that makes you proud.

Let's get the prospect of a bad grade out of the way, right now.

Imagine you're back in high school. You've made it past freshman year; you're a sophomore. You want to act like you know what you're doing, and you want to fit in. On the first day of school, your teacher enters the room—tall, serious, imposing. He's dressed formally, wears square glasses, and looks to be about the age of your parents. His presence commands the room. He has a reputation for having high standards, making kids work, and pushing them for results. His reputation precedes him; some of your friends have heard of him from their older siblings, and they have a healthy fear of him.

The first weeks in this teacher's class take on a pattern. Every day, he gives the class a quiz—five questions, one point each. They aren't too bad. Most days, you get three or even four answers right. You start to feel a bit confident.

And then, suddenly, it's time for the first test. You've heard about this teacher's tests; they are reputed to be harder than any in your other classes. As he begins passing out the booklets and answer forms, a hush falls over the room; you and your classmates are anxiously awaiting a glimpse of what you're sure will be a scorcher of a test.

The teacher notices the nervous squirming, and he stops. Looking all the kids in the eye, he says with emphasis: "This test is designed to *raise* your grade."

You wonder what in the world he means.

He says it again: "This test is designed to *raise* your grade."

Several kids turn pale. No one is reassured.

"Listen to me," he says. "I'm not setting you up to fail. I'm giving you an opportunity to become *better*. I'm asking you to work toward what you are capable of doing. I know you're not wimps, and that's why I'm not treating you like wimps. I believe you have what it takes to ace this test."

Something occurs to you for the first time: *He takes you seriously.*

He's on your side.

We've all met teachers like this. Maybe it was a second

grade reading tutor, a junior high math teacher, a high school cross country coach. Maybe the teacher was not yours, but your child's. Maybe it was an older person in your family—an uncle, a grandmother, or even one of your parents. Whoever the teacher was, you remember how it felt to be challenged and to come out on the other side, having done more than you thought you were capable of doing.

In my case, the teacher was Karl Hauck, and he taught me American history in my sophomore year. Though intimidated at first, I grew to like him so much that senior year I enrolled in his Advanced Placement United States History class, one of the most demanding in the school. I loved it—mostly because he worked at it, he invited me to work at it, and I knew he was on my side.

I have carried Mr. Hauck's approach into the writing of this book, and have deployed it across these pages. This book is designed to raise your grade when navigating the world of trusts and family enterprise ownership. Think of the book as your personal tutor, your confidence tool to handle the Integrity Problem. I believe you have what it takes to solve this problem. I know you are a future-minded, curious, honest family leader who wants to make sure your situation and your family's situation go well.

This book is designed to be practical. At the end of each chapter, you will encounter quizzes—a set of five focus questions designed to help you take action on specific issues of trusts and ownership in your family. Answer the questions in whatever circumstances fit you best; by yourself, with your family, or with someone you trust. Don't be afraid to write in the book. Take as many notes as you like. You can't raise your grade if no one lets you practice.

Throughout this book, our focus will be ownership—ownership of any asset valuable enough that you want to pass it on. We will look closely at assets you co-own with others, especially people in your family, and especially assets owned in trust. By the time you finish this book, you will have learned what a trust is, what a trustee does, what family ownership has to do with you, how you might integrate a trust into your life, and how you can take charge of your life as an owner.

I have spent the last 20 years of my professional life helping families from multiple vantage points I have staked out—initially as attorney, then as family enterprise ownership advisor, and later as trust fiduciary. Having helped families owning everything from land to huge warehouses to clothes-making equipment, I can tell you: this work is interdisciplinary. One profession alone does not get the job done. That's why multiple vantage points are an advantage. Nor can one person alone get the job done. That's why you are best off if you have someone to talk to as you read and apply this book. Writing down your thoughts, and having substantive conversations, are your two most powerful tools.

Whether you realize it or not, you *are* an owner. It's time to develop your confidence as one.

CHAPTER ONE

THE IMPLICATIONS OF OWNERSHIP

"The eye is the first circle; the horizon which it forms is the second. And throughout nature this primary figure is repeated without end."

—RALPH WALDO EMERSON, 1841

Some years ago, I found myself driving into a small Midwestern town to meet the second-generation family owners of a specialty manufacturing business. Their office occupied an old brick building that looked like a granary. The building lay at the end of an unmarked street, and neither the street nor the building had any signage. If the owners had not given me explicit directions, I never would have found the place. In fact, if not for my reason for visiting them, I never would have imagined any significant business at all was being transacted on this obscure spot.

Yet this building was the center of something big. The business made simple products that people around the world used (and still use) every day. The company was international, with manufacturing plants in six American cities and operations in four foreign countries. You might think a company with this scale and spread would be a household name, but it was quite the opposite—very few people would know it. The company was a huge financial success, partly because it traded on obscurity. Within its specialized area of focus, the company had acquired most of its few competitors; it now held 90% market share in the United States.

Its leaders had developed an ingenious, self-perpetuating operations cycle. Under the company's standard contract with its retail users, when the original products wore out, the company retrieved them, brought them back to the factory, reconditioned them with replacement components, and sent them out again to be used once more. In this way, the company had made itself and its products the center of an entire industry worldwide.

Upon meeting the owners, I had to wonder if they realized they were *also* at the center—the center of the business. They enjoyed their work, they took pride in the business they were building, and mostly they enjoyed each other. But did they appreciate what it meant to be at the center as an owner?

You are reading this book because you are at the center, whether you realize it or not. To explain, let's take the example of a business—not because you necessarily own or work in a family business, but because a business is a clear way to see the point.

INITIAL CIRCLES

In the manufacturing business I was asked to visit, four siblings were the owners—two brothers, two sisters. Their parents had died, and they were carrying on an enterprise their mother had started. All four worked in the business and received their sole paychecks from the business. All four were married, and all had children. Four households depended on the business to bring in an income, buy food, pay bills, set aside money for vacations, and save for the future.

THE NEXT RING OF CIRCLES

But many more households were involved. Several dozen people worked at the old brick headquarters. Each of those people received a paycheck. Most were married, and nearly all of them had households of more than one person. They too depended on the business to bring in an income. They spent their earnings at grocery stores, clothing stores, gas stations, restaurants, schools, and parks in the town and surrounding areas. In turn, each store where they spent their paychecks employed people, and those people also had households.

THE OUTWARD CIRCULAR EFFECT

That's just in the small town where the company ran its main office. Remember, this company had manufacturing plants in multiple cities, in the United States and in Europe. In each location, the same dynamic took place: the employees took their wages and spent, saved, invested, and donated the proceeds to the benefit of their own households, their extended families, other businesses, and charitable organizations.

Plus, the company held contracts with large retail users of its products. Most of these retailers had thousands of employees, each with a household, who spent their earnings in this same pattern in the respective places where they lived.

From this one business, dozens of concentric circles rippled out, each with its own set of interconnections. The owners had never stopped to count the circles. If they did, they probably would have undercounted the number of people across the world who in some way were tied to the activities of the business this family owned.

If not for this one business, in this one old building on an unmarked street in this one Midwestern town, and if not for the four siblings owning and working in this business, none of these concentric circles would have existed. No person would have occupied them in this same way, in this same set of interconnections, forming these particular human relationships.

THE CIRCLES AND FAMILY CAPITAL

The interconnections that come from the rippling circles reflect an owner's use of capital. We're not talking about just financial capital—money, land, building, equipment, lines of credit, things like that. Any owner, and any enterprise-owning family, has capital far beyond money. There is human capital: the people who comprise your family. There is intellectual capital: what each member of your family knows. There is social capital: the relationships you and your family have with each other and people in the places where the circles ripple. And there is spiritual capital: your family's shared intentions, humility, and views and pursuit of the ultimate things.[13]

These other forms of capital drive your financial capital. In fact, there's a good case to be made that long-term in your family, the human capital and the intellectual capital are more important than the financial. We'll take a closer look at this question in Chapter 7.

Here's a diagram, based on the company I visited, that shows the effect of the ownership circles we've just considered. In this example, the four owners are in the center, surrounded immediately by the employees at the headquarters. Surrounding this set of relationships are concentric circles for four manufacturing plants – in Texas, New Jersey, Ireland, and Minnesota

13 James E. Hughes, Jr., Susan E. Massenzio, and Keith Whitaker, *Complete Family Wealth* (Wiley 2018), pp. 11-12.

– and two branch offices – in California and France. Each plant and branch office has its own employees, who affect the local economy of each place and create their own sets of relationships.

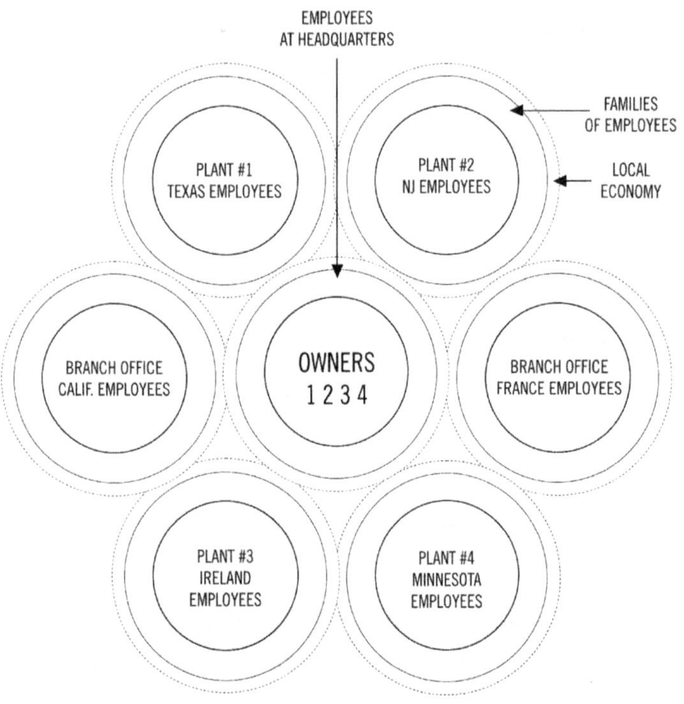

CHAPTER ONE

IDEAS BRING ABOUT THE CIRCLES

The circles of ownership don't ripple out on their own. They ripple out because someone has a good idea. In the business I visited, that good idea was a product people used every day, and reconditioning the product when it wore out.

Good ideas don't arise on their own. They arise through people. Take my friend Gary, who grew up in a trailer and cleaned floors at the local Wendy's restaurant. Gary had a knack for seeing and understanding how systems worked, so eventually he bought his own franchise restaurant. Then he bought another one. In the meantime, he completed college, became an accountant, worked in operations of a professional services firm, and earned a law degree. He liked accounting, but his favorite idea was a restaurant system he had developed. He put this idea to work creating a restaurant company.

Today, Gary's company operates dozens of franchise restaurants in cities across the Mid-South. The customers are happy, and the restaurants make money. But the most significant result of Gary's idea, and after Gary the next wave of circles rippling outward, is the advancement of the employees. Gary has a knack for helping blue collar workers see a bigger future. He prefers to promote from within. Many people who started on the line in the kitchen now have the responsibilities of store managers, regional managers, and corporate managers. In exercising their responsibilities, each of those employees has generated circles of their own. In each city where there's a store, the employees have created a set of interconnections rippling outward.

PEELING BACK TO THE CENTER

Now let's look at you. You may not feel you are at the center of anything. You may not feel you own much of anything. If you are engaged in a business, you may feel you're simply doing your job. If you're not in a business, you may not feel any real connection to the family trust or investments of which you somehow are an owner.

And yet, you *are* an owner. That puts you at the center.

One reason it's hard to see yourself at the center is that often someone else receives recognition for you being there. If you own an enterprise started by someone in a generation prior to you, other people may look to your ancestor as the one who did something important. If you co-own a piece of real estate with your sister but you do not physically work on the real estate, other people may think you do not "do anything." If you are a beneficiary of a trust you did not create, other people may look to the trust creator as the one who "had all the money." You may feel overlooked and undervalued.

Ownership poses tricky questions. For one thing, it makes you come face to face with money—money you created, as well as money you did not create but you have access to, such as by inheritance or marriage. Ownership also makes you consider whether you will fail or succeed with what you own, to the extent you control it. It makes you consider what "success" means. How will you know you have been successful in your ownership?

CONFRONTING THE INTEGRITY PROBLEM

Finally, and most of all, ownership prompts the bottom-line question: *where is my life going?*

Between me and the thing I own, does my life have integrity? Have I integrated this thing I own into my life? Does this thing fit with the rest of my life, or is it simply a foreign object that happens to occupy space adjacent to me?

Ownership presents fundamentally a question of integrity. Again, calling it the Integrity Problem does not mean anyone is dishonest or corrupt. It means a person who is an owner faces a special challenge in becoming whole and undivided. It's the challenge of integrating what you own and who you are. This challenge is not simple, and it doesn't square away quickly. The four siblings on the unmarked street wrestled with it. Gary and his employees wrestle with it every day. It's the same challenge you face. They're meeting the challenge.

So can you.

FOCUS QUESTIONS

1. Identify the circles that surround you at the center as the owner. If you own a business, for example, these could be your business's location and the people who work there; if you don't own a business, these could be relationships you have due to ownership of what you own.

2. Who are the people in these circles who exercise influence over your ownership?

3. What ideas created these circles? What was the driving idea behind what you own? What made the enterprise "go", which resulted in your ownership?

4. How much do you feel you have integrated what you own into who you are?

5. What are the three biggest challenges you face in integrating what you own and who you are?

CHAPTER TWO

A FAMILY ENTERPRISE

"My brother and I had fished the Big Blackfoot since nearly the beginning of the century—my father before then. We regarded it as a family river, as a part of us..."

—NORMAN MACLEAN, A RIVER RUNS THROUGH IT

If someone asked you to define the word "owner," what would you say?

Using the broadest definition, your mind might leap immediately to simple ownership of objects. For example, you own a car. What distinguishes you as the "owner" from someone else as a non-owner? It's not just the use of it; your teenagers might use the car to get to school, but they don't *own* it. No, the distinguishing factor is agency: you as the owner decide what happens to the car, who uses it, and whether it is registered, kept, or sold—whether its value is transmuted from *functional* value to *economic* value. The car is subject to your authority.

Let's take that definition, then, and narrow our focus to

business. Who is the "owner" of a business? Is it simply a person who has a say in what happens in the business and whether it is kept or sold? Not really, because in addition to operating the business, there is the aspect of the *proceeds* from the business that distinguishes ownership. You might add to the definition and reply that an "owner" is also a person who derives value from a business and owns the proceeds.

Then there's the question of employment. Would you limit "owner" to a person who works in the business? Would you say that, if they don't work in the business, they're not owners?

Beyond that is the timing of ownership. Does ownership always require an active, ongoing business? If your family no longer has an ongoing family business, are you an owner? For example, if your family sold its business 30 years ago and you and your relatives have access to cash invested from the sale, are you still owners?

The answer is that all these definitions reveal some truth about ownership. Yes, when you are an owner, you hold authority over what you own. Yes, when you own a business, you receive the proceeds of the business's operations. Yes, when you're an owner who also works in the business, you're more than an employee. And yes, if your family sold the business years ago and has invested the proceeds, you're still an owner of those proceeds. In each case, you are most certainly an owner.

And yet, ownership involves more than each of these answers. To see why, and to take a comprehensive approach to these questions, consider this definition:

> An owner is someone who has rights to the economic value of a thing owned, subject to restraints imposed by legal agreements and expectations of family, including those who came before you and those who come after you.[14]

An owner is someone who not only has rights *to* a thing owned—the agency to decide what happens to it—but also rights to the economic value of a thing owned. In the case of a business, its shape in your life once it is sold is filled with the economic value it leaves behind. Your ownership does not evaporate simply because the format of this economic value has changed. The value remains, and you remain an owner who both benefits from it and decides what happens to it.

Here are the three most important aspects of the quoted definition: (1) economic value; (2) family expectations; and (3) family members who come before or after you. Let's take a quick look at each.

ECONOMIC VALUE

There is far more to being an owner than simply extracting money from a thing you own. People own things for plenty of reasons not connected directly to money. They own for reasons

14 Modifies a definition by Ken McCracken, *The Alternative Family Business Dictionary* (2022).

of circumstance, beauty, convenience, sentiment, or simple personal attachment.

But economic value is an essential feature of being an owner. If there is no economic value at all—that is, if the thing owned does not have, and never will have, any value of any kind in the marketplace—then it may be an object you possess, but most people would not say you are an owner of it. Being an owner implies that the thing you own has some economic value, to you and other people.

Remember, though, that economic value does not sit by itself. It is not divorced from the other types of value, or capital, you find in a family: human capital, intellectual capital, social capital, spiritual capital. Economic value is part of the glue that binds you and your family together. But it's not the *only* glue.

FAMILY EXPECTATIONS

When you are an owner, assuming you have family, the thing you own is bound up in restraints imposed by your family's expectations. Your family has opinions about whether the thing is valuable, attractive, beautiful, useful, practical. They have opinions about whether you should own it. They also have views on whether its economic value will benefit them—because they have expectations about what you will do with it. Your view of the thing owned is not the only view that matters. The views of your family also matter.

You may fear your family's views about what you own, and about what you co-own with them. As we will see in this book, when dealing with ownership, courage is required. You and your family are on a journey together, and you cannot afford to be immobilized by fear of that journey and the challenges it presents. You need to have real conversations with your co-owners, and you need courage to hold these conversations.[15]

FAMILY BEFORE AND AFTER YOU

Your family members whose views matter are not just those in your immediate household. The group includes certain people who preceded you in life and certain people who come after you. They include people such as your grandparents, your parents, your aunts and uncles, your brothers and sisters, your cousins, your children, your grandchildren, your nieces and nephews.

Not all of these people will matter for everything you own. Some of them will matter very much—for example, your sister who is a beneficiary of a trust with you, or your son who wants to keep the vacation property in the family after you die. Others will matter less, especially if you have no economic tie to them. The point is simply that you are part of a chain much larger than you, a set of family relationships much more exten-

15 Susan Scott, *Fierce Conversations: Achieving Success at Work and in Life, One Conversation at a Time* (Berkley 2017), p. 194.

sive than you. Your family is making its way through time, and right now you are in the middle of it. You are taking your turn at the wheel.

AN 'ENTERPRISE'

Some things you own by yourself—for example, your car. Other things you own with other people—for example, a joint checking account or a house. An enterprise is simply another type of thing you own with other people, though with layers and dimensions.

By "enterprise" I mean all assets, activities, and entities through which the lives of family members are connected.[16]

Let's repeat that. An enterprise means *all assets, activities, and entities through which the lives of family members are connected.*

Assets, activities, entities—these are the points of connection for an enterprising family. These are the ways people in your family are tied together. Recall the phrase from our definition of ownership: an owner is "subject to restraints imposed by legal agreements and expectations of family". You don't co-own in a vacuum; you co-own within a governing structure. Think of it like your car; unless it's a collectible that sits pristine in a garage or showroom, you don't own a car with no governing as-

16 I am indebted to Ken McCracken, the leading family business ownership advisor in the United Kingdom, for this definition. He made me aware of it, and I have not found a better one.

pects like a license plate or registration that enable you to drive it down the road. The same is true of a family enterprise; it is subject to a governing structure that involves points of connection. The points of connection can be quite simple, but they create the fabric of ownership.

Here are examples of each of these points of connection:

- Assets:
    - Cash in a trust account, resulting from sale of a successful investment 30 years ago
    - Stock dividends, received every year from stocks a trust owns
    - Land owned by four cousins that never has been developed
    - Customer contracts in a family warehousing business
- Activities:
    - A job in a family metal recycling business
    - A fishing trip every year with your uncles to a cabin at a 125-year-old fishing club
    - Giving money to local charities in December
- Entities:
    - A trust that pays for healthcare emergencies and education for grandchildren
    - A limited liability company that owns apartments

- A donor-advised fund that makes grants to a local food bank at Thanksgiving

TYPES OF ENTITIES

This third point of connection, entities, bears a further look. Many people think of an ownership entity as simply a business. As you can see by now, there's more to it than that. In fact, there are four common types of entities.

First is an *operating company*, an entity that family members run to earn a living and provide jobs for themselves. Most commonly an operating company is a family business, such as a family manufacturing or distribution company.

Second is a *family investment*, an entity that holds cash and other assets owned in common. For example, the investment might be apartment buildings that churn out rental income every month for a father and his two sons. Some might contend the investment isn't exactly a family business, since no family members work in it; but it's an important and valuable thing for the family.

Third is property *not* owned primarily to generate a return. The most common example is family vacation property. It might be worth a lot of money (and its value increases over time), yet you own it not primarily because you seek to eventually tap its market value. You own it because it's a place where your family gathers to spend leisure time together. Its value is not just economic worth but emotional connection. It's a place where memories are made and where the passage of time in a family is marked.

Finally, the fourth entity type is a *charitable entity*, such as money held in a donor advised fund or a private foundation. It exists to give money on a charitable basis to people who need help. The value of this entity also extends beyond the economic value of the money. With this entity, you as the person responsible for it are a part of something bigger than yourself. You're helping support your community and you're helping build its future.

MORE THAN YOU THOUGHT

When you keep in mind the three aspects of a family enterprise—assets, activities, entities—and the four types of entities—operating company, family investment, family property, charitable entity—you see the vastness of the range of possible enterprises.

From this vantage point, you see that a family enterprise is not the same as a family business. A family enterprise is broader and reaches potentially farther than an operating company. A family enterprise touches more parts of a family's life as the family moves through time; it connects the past, present, and future through the assets, entities, and activities that make up its structure.

If you co-own anything with other people in your family, or if you have present or future rights connected to the co-ownership, you are not just the owner of a property or a business. You are involved in a family enterprise, and your ownership demands action.

This raises an important question:

Why in the world would you want to be involved in this way with other people in your family?

It's a great question, and it's the subject of the next chapter.

FOCUS QUESTIONS

1. **Under the definition of "Owner" in this chapter, what are the three most important things you own?**

2. **What are your favorite family assets?**

3. **Which family activities do you enjoy the most?**

4. **Which family entities most connect the lives of people in your family?**

5. **Of the four types of entities identified in this chapter, which ones are most central to who you are and what you do?**

CHAPTER THREE

WHY OWN TOGETHER?

"It seems to have been reserved to the people of this country, by their conduct and example, to decide the important question, whether societies of human beings are really capable or not, of establishing good government from reflection and choice, or whether they are forever destined to depend, for their political constitutions, on accident and force."

—THE FEDERALIST NO. 1, OCTOBER 27, 1787

Which way do you prefer to make decisions—by reflection and choice, or by accident and force?

When deciding something important, do you prefer to have time to think and to choose for yourself? Or are you comfortable deciding in light of an accident, or because someone forces you to agree?

This is not a hard question to answer; no one wants to be in the second category. Everyone wants to be in the first. Everyone prefers to make decisions with time to reflect and by their own choice—deciding because they want to, not because someone else *made* them.

Everyone wants to decide for themselves about things they own. It's one of the privileges of ownership; you as an owner get to decide what happens to the thing you own. People prefer to decide for themselves whether to own something, what to own, how long to own it, with whom to own it, and how to dispose of it when the ownership ends. No matter what you own, you do not want someone else ordering you around.

Co-ownership with family members is no different. All family members want to decide for themselves the terms on which they will own something with a parent, a sibling, a cousin. This desire is natural. It is rooted deeply within each person.

A BETTER ANSWER THAN 'FAMILY DYNAMICS'

And yet, as every family knows, the desire to decide for one's self sometimes gives rise to disagreement. One family member decides in favor of one outcome; the other decides in favor of another. In some families, the disagreement turns into a total, permanent rift. The specter of such division may explain why many people have a hard time talking about family disagreements about co-ownership. They know something bad when they see it, but they lack a way to talk about it. As a result, they also lack a way to think about it. Like onlookers at the scene of a car accident, rather than bothering to understand the injuries, they stand by and murmur among themselves about how bad the collision was.

For example, people often describe a family ownership disagreement as bound up in "family dynamics." By this, they mean some kind of whirling cloud of inexplicable forces at work in the family—something formless and beyond description. They use this expression because they have no framework for analyzing the disagreement, and because it's how they've heard other people characterize the problem. "Family dynamics" is a safe, blameless phrase, one that removes responsibility from the family members in question. It's also an unfortunate way of pathologizing a family by slapping a label on its members: "Oh, you've heard about the messy problems in *that family*. It's family dynamics." When a family is depicted in this way, the depiction robs the family members of the agency they can exercise to improve their situation.

Even professionals talk this way. You might hear the expression "family dynamics" come out of the mouth of the very expert—an attorney, an investment advisor, an accountant—whom you expected would know *how* to deal with the whirling cloud. There's a reason for this: experts who fall back on "family dynamics" do so because they're out of their element. They don't have a process for helping the family through the disagreement. Maybe the expert's professional training did not equip him or her with tools for handling the problem. Maybe the expert's fee structure does not create margin for dealing with co-ownership difficulties. Maybe the expert simply does not have the stomach for this kind of problem. Regardless, when you hear this expression, you feel stuck.

You, the co-owner, don't need to feel stuck. You don't need to live your life hijacked by the vagaries of "family dynamics." If you and your co-owners are not aligned, that's okay. Be honest about the lack of alignment. Then deal with it systematically.

How do you begin to deal with it? The best place to start is Shared Purpose.

SHARED PURPOSE

Shared Purpose is the unique mix of reasons you and your co-owners own something together.[17] It explains *why* you and they are willing to be owners together. It's the glue that holds you and your co-owners together—to each other, and to what you own. It's the set of outcomes you and your co-owners use to measure the overall success of your family and what you own.

Shared Purpose reminds you that ownership, especially ownership with other people, is a choice.[18] You are free to own together with other people, and you are free not to. No one is forcing you to be a co-owner. You may feel pressured to do it, and in that case your decision is not genuine. You also may not have uncovered the real reasons you want to be a co-owner. You may not yet have explored the basis for a choice. The choice

17 See McCracken, *The Alternative Family Business Dictionary*, p. 56.

18 Amelia Renkert-Thomas, *Engaged Ownership* (Wiley 2016), pp. 85-87.

awaits you. You, a person at the center, need to make it. And you are the only one who can make it.

Shared Purpose is fundamental. Without Shared Purpose, fights among owners are nearly guaranteed. This is because the various owners will seek different outcomes from the same thing that is owned, and inevitably these outcomes will not align.

Don't let the prospect of fighting discourage you. The remedy is a Shared Purpose, and it has four elements:[19]

1. **Shared Vision.** The co-owners share goals they seek to achieve by owning the asset.
2. **Shared Morals.** The co-owners share a sense of right and wrong.[20]
3. **Shared Mission.** The co-owners agree on the actions they need to pursue in order to achieve their shared goals in a way consistent with their shared morals.
4. **Shared Life Aspirations.** The co-owners hope to achieve certain things in life by owning the asset together.

Bear in mind three things about Shared Purpose. First, Shared Purpose is about more than money. As you examine your Shared Purpose, you'll probably find it is not solely eco-

19 I derived this list from an earlier version created by colleagues Ken McCracken and Amelia Renkert-Thomas.

20 Some might speak of this element in terms of "Shared Values," but I find "Shared Morals" to be more accurate. This element pertains to the owners' standards of good and bad, and as such it is essentially moral.

nomic. It may not even be primarily economic. It probably includes non-financial goals such as deepening family relationships and recognizing family history.

Second, Shared Purpose is natural, not artificial. It inheres among you and your co-owners. You can't fake it. For that matter, you can't manufacture it, as though it were a product. As we will see in Chapter 6, Shared Purpose draws upon natural abilities inherent in you and each of your co-owners. Nothing about it is contrived.

Third, because Shared Purpose involves human beings, it is an imperfect standard that aspires to be realistic. Shared Purpose does not demand perfection. Instead, Shared Purpose calls you, and each of your co-owners, to decide what you will live with and what you will live without. The standard for Shared Purpose is the Good Enough Standard.[21] It measures whether the Shared Purpose is "good enough."

THE GOOD ENOUGH STANDARD

To reach the Good Enough Standard, you answer these questions:

1. Is the Shared Purpose being proposed right for me? Does it fit me? Does it advance what I need?

21 I credit Ken McCracken for first characterizing the standard in this way.

2. Does it suit our family—not just me but other people in the family, especially those with whom I am a co-owner?
3. Is the Shared Purpose feasible in the real world? Assuming we all really want to make it happen, is it attainable?
4. Is it feasible in our enterprise—our enterprise being the assets we own, the activities we undertake, and the entities we use to hold the assets and make decisions?[22] Will this Shared Purpose work with our mix of assets and ownership structures?

If the answer to all four of these questions is "yes," you and your co-owners have arrived at a Shared Purpose. You've found the glue that holds you together. You know *why* you want to be owners together. You have lighted a path for all of you to travel, where you make decisions together based on reflection and choice, not accident and force. You will have answered the first important question.

SHARED PURPOSE AND THE INTEGRITY PROBLEM

When co-owners articulate a Shared Purpose, they tackle the Integrity Problem head-on. Each co-owner starts to see how he or she, combined with the other owners, become part of a

22 See Chapter 2 for the definition of family "enterprise."

whole. By combining with other co-owners to make a whole, each owner comes to terms with the money that pertains to him or her. A statement of Shared Purpose integrates what each owner owns with who they are.

Here are some quotes, derived from real family situations, of how family members might characterize their Shared Purpose:

- "When we kids were growing up, we ate dinner at one table—all of us together, even though there were so many bodies. We want to create new occasions where we keep doing that."

- "Our ownership is our choice and our chance. Each of us, and each generation, must decide for itself not just whether we continue owning together but how we can improve on what was done prior to us."

- "We are following the example of service our parents set. Dad used to restore salvage items for the poor. He volunteered at church fundraisers. Mom gave of herself to us."

- "To our surprise, we have created a forum where we are able to talk to each other constructively, even as the next generation expands and some of us work in the business."

- "Our personalities differ, yet we are aligned on the core value that our enterprise creates for people who deal with us. Our alignment moderates the disappointments and frustrations we inevitably will experience in our work."

- "This is our way to have peace, unity, and an understanding of individual needs. It's not the only way, but it's our way."

These snippets represent how real families actually talk to each other about their lives as co-owners. The discussions tend to be genuinely positive because as the family members talk, they realize they have more in common than they thought. They enter the room afraid to find out how much they disagree. They stay in the room relieved to discover how much they agree.

But for some, before they can say what they really think and how they really feel, they must surmount a self-worth obstacle.

SELF-WORTH AND THE INTEGRITY PROBLEM

When you are in the room for a Shared Purpose discussion, you are there for a crucial reason: you have something to contribute in fashioning the Shared Purpose. Yet you may not feel you have anything to contribute. You may feel unqualified—because the thing you own came about due to the work of family members who came before you. You may feel you are simply shepherding someone else's dream. Until now, no one may ever have asked you if you have your own dream about being a co-owner. You may have trouble articulating your thoughts. A deep feeling of unworthiness may impair your ability to contribute to the discussion.

Shared Purpose involves combining dreams of people in addition to yours—not just dreams of each of your co-owners, but also dreams of people who came before you and dreams of people who will come after you. Yet the pertinent point in time is now. We are talking about the present. What is *your* dream for what you own that drives *your* contribution to the Shared Purpose?[23]

You may be tempted to take your focus off of *your* role in creating the Shared Purpose and *your* dream behind *your* contribution. You may feel you need to justify having a dream of your own. You may even feel you need to apologize for calling it a dream. The word "dream" strikes some people the wrong way; to them it sounds imprecise, airy, vacuous, childish. If they don't relate to the word "dream," say you have an aspiration, an ambition, a vision for your future. After all, that's the point: you have a vision for a bigger future, and within it lies your contribution to the Shared Purpose.

---

23 For an eloquent analysis of the concept of the dream behind the co-ownership, see James E. Hughes Jr., Susan E. Massenzio and Keith Whitaker, *Complete Family Wealth (Bloomberg 2018),* p. 40, and *Hughes, Family: The Compact Among Generations (Bloomberg 2007),* pp. 189-195.

You must develop the confidence to come to terms with your dream and articulate your contribution. Developing this confidence is not easy. So many circumstances conspire to spook you. See them for what they are, and then navigate your way around them.

Here are two examples.[24]

'MY FATHER WOULD BE SO ASHAMED AT HOW THIS TURNED OUT.'

When Colleen said this, she was at the lowest point of coming to terms with her family. Colleen's grandfather had founded a specialty manufacturing business. Everything about the business was unsexy—the gritty assembly line, the old building, the noise, the rumbling of trucks in the shipping yard. Perhaps for this reason, Colleen's father had split ownership of the business into voting and nonvoting stock, with the women, Colleen and her three sisters, holding nonvoting stock only, and the man, Colleen's only brother Ted, owning all the voting stock. Ted, inexperienced and overconfident, was having a hard time earning the respect of his coworkers. When the children's father died suddenly, all five children went into a tailspin.

As life at the company worsened, Colleen was haunted by what her father would have thought of the mess. But first,

24 Except for several examples used with client permission, which are noted in the footnotes, all examples in this book are derivative of actual family situations, and no example is meant to depict a specific person or family.

she had to decide that her own dream was in fact to run the business, and that her dream fit what her father had wanted. She had to reconcile her opinion of the path forward with her perception of her father's vision for the business and his vision for her. Ultimately, she realized what people outside the family had been telling her for years: she was her father's daughter. This realization enabled Colleen to arrive, with her siblings, at a Shared Purpose that resulted in her becoming the president and running the business.

'JUST REMEMBER, THAT'S YOUR FATHER-IN-LAW'S MONEY.'

Ruth received this warning from her father-in-law's investment advisor. Ruth's father-in-law had sold a distribution business 15 years ago. By now, Ruth and her husband, Jeff, were in middle age. After selling the business, Ruth's father-in-law deployed some of the sale proceeds to an irrevocable trust that benefited both Jeff and Ruth. Though Jeff got along well with his father, and Ruth felt her father-in-law trusted her, neither Jeff nor Ruth was allowed to be a trustee of the trust. Nor did the father-in-law explain why he had set up the trust or what he hoped from it for Jeff, Ruth, and their children. Ruth found the investment advisor's statement demeaning. She felt the investment advisor viewed her not as a beneficiary of an important trust but as an in-law who had nothing to offer. Ruth had a hard time talking to her husband about a dream for distributions from the trust. She felt like a second-class citizen.

THE E WORD

Sometimes, discussions of Shared Purpose include the word no one likes to hear about themselves: *entitlement*. No one wants to hear that someone in the family views them as entitled. The specter of entitlement—to money, influence, control, status—imprisons a person, regardless of whether the person actually behaves as entitled. This is what happened to Colleen and Ruth. Colleen worried her father had given her only nonvoting shares because he viewed her as entitled. Ruth, for her part, was sure the financial advisor viewed her as entitled. Both Colleen and Ruth became imprisoned.

The real problem with entitlement is its causes, not its symptoms. The truth about entitlement is this:

> . . . The real cause of entitlement is the failure of the rising generation [in a family] to individuate. The core of entitlement is failing to see yourself as a capable, independent person. The antidote to entitlement is individuation.[25]

The root problem is self-perception. It's a matter of how you view yourself. If you view yourself as having no capabilities

25 James E. Hughes, Jr., *Complete Family Wealth*, p. 43.

of your own, if you see yourself as unable to act independently of your co-owners, you will be more likely to become entitled. You'll be more likely to come across as entitled. If, on the other hand, you see the capabilities you can develop and you see how you can exercise independence, entitlement will not appeal to you.

To be clear: neither Colleen nor Ruth actually behaved as people who were entitled to money or ownership. Neither sat around waiting for an inheritance. The problem was not that Colleen and Ruth were entitled or that they acted like they were. Instead, the real problem was that they were afraid of other people in their family *thinking* they were entitled. At critical points in their ownership journeys, this fear delayed them from taking steps toward being fully capable and independent.

THE THREE-CIRCLE MODEL

One very effective way to see Shared Purpose relationships in a family enterprise is to depict them on paper using a diagram. Called the "Three-Circle Model," the diagram shows how family, owners, and management are related in an enterprise.[26] Here's what the diagram looks like.

26 John Davis and Renato Taguiri, Harvard working paper, 1982, reprinted in "Bivalent Attributes of the Family Firm," *Family Business Review*, Vol. 9, No. 2 (1996). The Three-Circle Model has been used for over 40 years. Some in the field have criticized it as inadequate. The model continues to prevail, and is used in this book, because it shows things that are true.

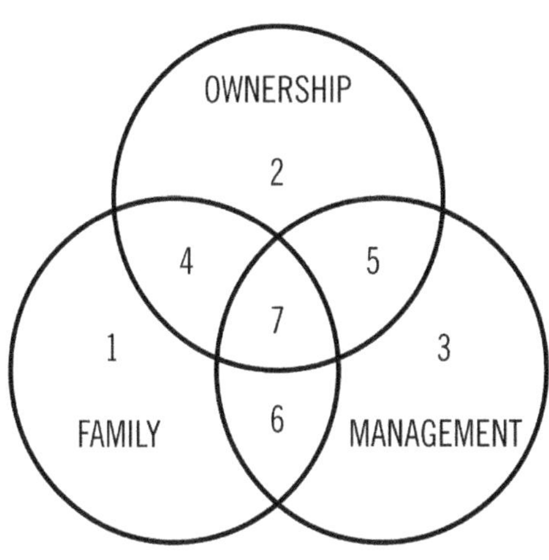

KEY NUMBER	KEY DESCRIPTION
1	**FAMILY MEMBERS** Not owners and not employees
2	**NON-FAMILY INVESTORS** Banks, non-bank lenders, private equity holders
3	**NON-FAMILY EMPLOYEES** Not family and not owners
4	**FAMILY OWNERS** But do not work for the enterprise
5	**NON-FAMILY WORKING OWNERS** Hold ownership in the enterprise, but are not family
6	**FAMILY EMPLOYEES** Non-owner family members who work for the enterprise
7	**WORKING FAMILY OWNERS** Family members who both own and work in or manage the enterprise

As you see, the three circles overlap. In the top center is the circle of owners of the enterprise. In the lower left is the circle of family members related to the enterprise. In the lower right is the circle of managers who oversee or operate the enterprise.

As the overlapping indicates, not all owners are necessarily family members. Not all family members operate the enterprise. And not all workers in the enterprise are owners or are family.

The Three-Circle Model elicits Shared Purpose in several ways. First, the diagram helps family members understand conflict. When you see where others are on the diagram, you understand why they might be upset. For example, if your sister does not individually own any of the family acreage, you are not surprised that being in the family circle but not the ownership circle troubles her.

Second, the diagram enables family members to see where they might move in the future and how future moves could develop their ownership. For example, if you are age 30 and in both the family and management circles, and you aspire to move to the center of all three circles, you will start developing the capabilities to serve in these mixed capacities. As you develop new capabilities, the odds of others seeing you as "entitled" will go down.

The Three-Circle Model originated in the world of family business, not the world of trusts and estate planning. As a result, the diagram does not show a clear or obvious place for family trusts. This omission actually proves the strength of the model, for depending on the trust, a trustee may appear in several different places on the model. We'll have more on this in Chapter 5. For now, the point is simply that the Three-Circle Model depicts the many places where Shared Purpose may arise in a family enterprise.

THE RESPONSIBLE OWNER™

One of the mysteries of co-ownership, and probably the single most frustrating question for family owners, is this: *Who really is in charge?* Who really owns the asset? Are you in charge of just your little corner of the co-owned world? Are you more in charge than you feel? Are you even less in charge than you feel? How can you know for sure?

This question becomes even more mysterious, and certainly more frustrating, when a trust is involved. A trust exists because someone wanted to create it. Someone established the trust. Yet, as we will see in the next chapter, that someone might not be the legal owner of the trust. And that someone probably is not the primary person whom the trust benefits. Of these three types of people—the person who set up the trust, the person who is the trust's legal owner, and the person whom the trust benefits—who is in charge of what? To what extent is any of them an owner? Does the trust seem like just one big, undifferentiated blobby mess?

Especially when the assets in your family enterprise consist of property you inherited, the question "Who is in charge?" becomes even more sharp. You did not bring to life the economic value you now enjoy. Someone who came before you did that. Yet you are a person at the center, and you have a great deal to do with how your family makes its way through time. What role do you play in this journey?

Multiple people can be authoritative at the same time. I jokingly refer to my wife as my immediate supervisor. I do not say she is my ultimate supervisor. That place belongs to another. But I do say, and I do mean seriously, that I feel responsible to her concerning our common life together. We have what lawyers might call a general partnership. We're all in on both the profits and the losses. There are no limitations. When something goes well, we're all in. When something bad happens, both of us are all in. Because I'm all in with her, I see her as authoritative. She's responsible for what happens, and so am I.

Similarly, with respect to what you co-own, you are a Responsible Owner.[27] The Responsible Owner is not the Ultimate Owner, a person who absolutely has the last word. But the Responsible Owner is the person on the scene, the person who takes care of what is owned, the person who integrates what is owned into his or her life. Some people call such person a "steward."

27 "Responsible Owner" is a trademark of The Family Enterprise Office, LLC. All rights reserved.

WHAT ABOUT GOD?

Speaking of an owner as a steward raises a deep question. So far in this book, we have hit touchy subjects: money, entitlement, family. Now it's time for another touchy subject: God. Or, if you prefer, the subject is human agency. What is your role in exercising authority over what you own? To what extent are you actually the ultimate owner of your assets?

As one prominent, entrepreneurial, and extremely successful investment advisor has put it, "God owns it all. My name may be attached to all the accounts and property under my control, but my name is on them only temporarily. I'm only a steward, and I'm going to leave it all behind." But, he adds, "I am able to choose the next steward."[28]

You need not be a member of a particular faith to see the significance of the question. At issue is human agency. Whether you are of a religious faith, or of uncertain faith, or of no faith, and yet at least of good faith, you recognize you are not a robot. You make many choices every day. The choices are real. How you make them affects you, your household, and those in your family who come after you. You, as a Responsible Owner, make choices.

One of those choices is: who will be the next steward? We'll have more on this question in Chapter 7.

28 Ron Blue, *Splitting Heirs* (Northfield Publishing 2004), p. 57.

In the meantime, recognize that if you aspire to have some involvement in deciding how you handle what you own, and if you aspire to handle it well, you are a Responsible Owner. You have a lot to do with how your ownership affects yourself and your family. You have a lot to do with how your family turns out.

THE RESPONSIBLE OWNER, IN CHARGE

To the question, "Who is in charge?," the answer is: you are, concerning certain aspects of what is owned.

To the question, "Who is the owner?," again the answer is: you are, concerning certain aspects of what is owned.

You really are an owner, and you really are in charge. You probably are not the sole owner, and you might not be the ultimate owner. But you are a Responsible Owner. You exercise authority over what you are responsible for—yourself, your own dreams, your household and those from it who come after you, your Shared Purpose with your co-owners, your faith, your future, and perhaps most of all, your confidence. Ultimately, confidence is why you own together with others in your family.

And to develop your confidence further, you need to understand how trusts relate to your family enterprise. In the next chapter, you're going to learn how.

FOCUS QUESTIONS

1. **What are some of the reasons you and your co-owners choose to own this enterprise together? What's your "why"?**

2. **Do you feel unworthy, unqualified, or without your own capabilities to be an owner? If so, why?**

3. **In creating a Shared Purpose with your co-owners, what's the most valuable contribution you can make?**

4. **Where are you located on the Three-Circle Model?**

5. **In what ways are you a Responsible Owner™?**

CHAPTER FOUR

HOW TRUSTS WORK

"We do not know very much of the future, except that from generation to generation, the same things happen again and again."

—T.S. ELIOT, MURDER IN THE CATHEDRAL

Have you ever felt like you don't know much about trusts?

If so, you're like most people. If you stood outside on the street and interviewed passers-by TV-talk-show-style, asking them what a trust is, nine out of ten would likely stare blankly into the camera and say a trust has something to do with lawyers. The tenth out of ten *might* be a business owner who can give you some detail. But in my experience, even some sophisticated business owners don't know a whole lot about trusts—what they're for, how they work, and how they're administrated and governed.

Some years ago, I was working on an ownership matter for a large family. Present at our meeting were four generations, about forty people in total. To make the meeting manageable, we divided the family by generation. In just one generation were enough people to fill out all four sides of a large square table.

As we sat down, I heard the man next to me—a key figure in this large family, and a person central to his generation—whisper to his wife, while gesturing toward his cousin across the table, "Who is my cousin's trustee?"

His wife whispered back to him, "Well, dummy, you are."

This family business was of significant size. Much of it was owned by trusts. Individual family members were the trustees. And this particular family member, who worked in the business and had helped it grow many times over, had no idea he was a trustee of a trust that owned a business worth a large number.

And yet, despite what his wife said, this man was no dummy. He was a successful executive in the company. He knew all about his compensation as an employee. He knew he owned stock in the business for himself. Yet he did not know he also was the legal owner of stock that benefited his cousin and his cousin's branch of the family.

Stunning knowledge gaps like this develop for a simple reason: people do not understand how a family trust works. And the reason people do not understand is equally simple: no one bothers to tell them.

That's what you're about to learn. By the end of this chapter, you will understand how a trust works.

OWNERSHIP IS THE KEY

If you take nothing else from this book, remember this one point:

A trust is a type of owner.

Think of it this way:

Some things you own in your own name. Take your car, for example. Unless your car is an asset of your business, your car is likely owned by you alone. When you go to the license agency Web site to renew your license plates, they ask you who owns the car, and you give them your name. Your car is an example of an asset you own individually, in your own name.

There are also things you own jointly with other people; for example, a joint checking account at a bank. Typically the owners are married spouses. Sometimes a parent will own a checking account with an adult child, so both of them have authority to pay bills from the account in case the parent becomes ill. A joint checking account is an example of an asset two people own together, in both their names.

A trust is simply another way of owning something. It's a more complicated way, but it's more complicated for a good and important reason.

THE HISTORY BEHIND TRUSTS

The reason comes from the purpose behind trusts. Trusts have existed for nearly 1,000 years. They originated in England, under English law. At that time, landowners needed to depart from their property for months at a time—to conduct business, to protect their country against intruding enemies, or to engage in war abroad. Being away from the property also meant leaving behind one's wife and family. (At that time, by law landowners were male only.) The landowner wanted to protect his family and all he owned, and he certainly did not want an outsider to take the property from him.[29]

An initial solution was to leave the property in the hands of a neighbor, relative, or friend, with instructions to protect the land and pay taxes. Putting such a person in charge did not always work. The difficulty was that in some cases, when the landowner returned, the interim owner did not want to give back the property.[30]

The resulting solution, devised by English courts of law, was to split the concept of ownership into two aspects: a legal owner and a beneficial owner. In the eyes of the law, one person was treated as the legal owner, who had authority to pay bills, take care of taxes, and maintain the property. The other person

29 Scott & Ascher on Trusts (6th ed.) (Wolters Kluwer 2019), §1.1; Patricia Angus, The Trustee Primer: A Guide for Personal Trustees (2016), pp. 3-5.

30 Angus, p. 4; Scott & Ascher, §1.2.

was the beneficial owner, the person whom the property was intended to benefit.[31]

Under this system of bifurcated ownership, the neighbor, relative or friend became the legal owner and took on the rights and responsibilities of maintaining the property. The wife and children became beneficial owners who had access to the property, could use the property, and received the benefits of the property.[32]

Neither the legal owner nor the beneficial owner had authority over all aspects of the trust. Both were owners, but in different respects. Each had their own sphere of ownership.

Five hundred years later, when English colonists began inhabiting North America, they brought with them the English legal tradition of trusts and bifurcated ownership. As the colonies grew, and when the United States of America was formed after the American Revolution, American law continued the English system of trusts.[33]

HOW SPLIT OWNERSHIP WORKS

Although modern American trust law differs in important ways from its English predecessor, the basics remain the same. Here's the personnel lineup:

31 Scott & Ascher, §1.1.

32 Scott & Ascher, §1.1; Angus, p. 5.

33 Scott & Ascher, §1.9.

Trust: A written agreement, a set of rules, explaining the administration, investment, and distribution of the property in the trust.

Grantor (sometimes called Settlor): The trust creator—the person who sets up the trust and contributes property to it. The property could be cash, stock, land, a personal residence, a car collection, a vacation place—just about anything you could imagine. If you can own it, you can put it in a trust.

Beneficiary: The person or people who receive income and principal from the trust. These are the first set of people you intend to benefit in setting up the trust. They are the beneficial owners of the property in the trust.

Remainder Person: A type of beneficiary. The person or people who receive the remainder at the end of the trust. These are the final people you intend to benefit in setting up the trust. They too are beneficial owners of the property, though they benefit later in time.

Trustee: The person or company that administers, invests, and distributes the property in the trust under the set of rules in the trust agreement. They are the legal owner of the property in the trust.

You can see each of these people on the Trust Triangle diagram that follows.

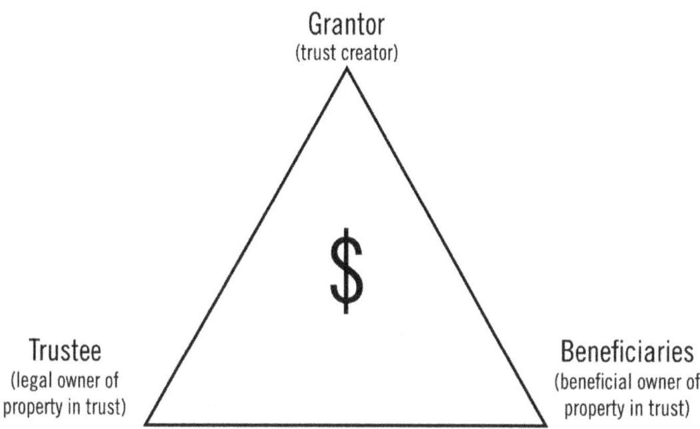

At the top angle is the grantor, the person who sets up the trust. In the lower left corner is the trustee, the person who is the legal owner of the trust. In the lower right corner are the beneficiaries, the people who are the beneficial owners of the trust.

Of all the people on this diagram, the most important is the beneficiary.

You might think the most important person is the grantor, who set up the trust. Or you might think the most important person is the trustee, who is legally responsible for the ownership structure.

But in fact, the most important person on the diagram is the beneficiary. Let's see why.

SOMEONE TO BENEFIT

Often people are told they need a trust for tax reasons. On the subject of trusts, lawyers enjoy talking expansively about taxes. Let's say you are a person who has, or expects to have, enough money that you could lose it to estate taxes. A trust, the lawyer tells you, will help manage your tax exposure.

Nearly as often, you are told you need a trust to keep the money safe from unreliable relatives. Privately you worry that your children, for example, waste money, have a poor work ethic, and can't get their act together. A trust, you are told, will protect the money from these developing problems.

Taxes and family—both of these may be reasons for creating a trust. But by themselves they don't get at the root of the issue.

The root truth is far simpler:

You create a trust because you are trying to *benefit* someone.

That someone may be yourself. It may be your spouse. It may be your children or your grandchildren. It may be all of you.

In every instance, you are trying to make someone better off. By providing for the person you seek to benefit, you are trying to express your regard, even love, for that person. You want the trust to show you love the person in question. You may not put it that way, and your advisors almost certainly will not speak of it that way, but that is in fact what ultimately is on your mind.

A trust is a legal expression of the regard you have for someone—how you feel about them, what you think of them.

It's as simple as that—and as complicated. Because you are trying to make someone better off, you necessarily are trying not to make that person *worse* off. (We'll talk more about that in Chapter 5.)

For now, let's stay focused on benefit. How exactly does a trust benefit someone?

SO WHERE'S THE BENEFIT?

How does a beneficiary receive, in a practical way, the benefit of the trust?

The short answer is: by receiving distributions. A distribution is the payment of money out of the trust to a beneficiary. Just as a beneficiary is the most important person in a trust, so distributions are the main feature of a trust. When you set up a trust, you place property in the trust because you expect the property to come out of the trust to be paid to a beneficiary. If you didn't think the property would ever come out, you wouldn't put it in. Otherwise you wouldn't be able to help the beneficiary.

A set of written rules, spelled out in a document called a trust agreement, governs how the property comes out. Typically the rules call for the property to come out in increments and over time. But the property does come out. The property is put in so it will come out.

Based on what the rules of the road in the trust agreement say, the trustee pays out property from the trust to the beneficiaries. Usually the distribution is cash; the trustee pays cash to the beneficiary. There are two types of distributions—payment of income, and payment of principal. In standard trusts, there are automatic payments of income, at least once per year. If the beneficiary needs more money than that, the trustee may have power to distribute principal, the base money in the trust that generates the interest income. In either case, the trustee pays out the money by taking it from the trust's investments. The trustee will pay the distribution to the beneficiary by check or electronic deposit. The money then belongs to the beneficiary. The beneficiary can spend the money, save the money, or both.

NOT AN ACCOUNT

Because a trust involves income and principal, you may get the impression a trust is simply an account. After all, trusts often own cash, stocks, and bonds, just like an investment account. Many investment advisory firms manage trust money as though it were simply another account.

For one family our firm assisted, the investment advisory firm had labeled the account as, "Daria Edison Trustee Daria

Edison Trust" (all one line, no commas).[34] After Mrs. Edison died at age 103, her son, who was her successor trustee, needed to deposit a refund check to her trust account. When he asked the investment advisory firm about depositing the check, the firm identified the payee as "Daria Edison Trustee Daria Edison Trust," disregarding the obvious fact that Daria Edison, being dead, no longer was the trustee. In the firm's eyes, the account and the trust were the same.

Do not let this confuse you. A trust is not an account. The trust is the *owner* of the account. The trust itself is not the account.

A trust is always connected to a person. When looking at property like bank accounts or investment accounts, always ask yourself: who *owns* this account? Who is the legal owner, and who is the beneficial owner? Who is the person behind the property? Asking the ownership question will help you keep straight who the person is and what the property is. The two are not the same.

HOW THE PEOPLE TURN OUT

Because a trust makes money available to beneficiaries at a certain time, under certain standards, and for certain reasons, the trust affects how the beneficiary turns out. Parents care how their children turn out. So too a person who sets up a trust

34 The name here is fictitious, but this example really happened.

cares—or should care—how the beneficiaries turn out. "Turning out" involves upside potential as much as downside risk. Downside is not the only side. Trust creators commonly worry about the beneficiaries becoming "trust fund babies," people who are excessively dependent on the money in the trust. This fear turns into a specter, because no one tells the trust creator about cases where a trust has done a lot of good for its beneficiaries.[35] In fact, when designed and implemented carefully, a trust contains potential for tremendous upside. We will cover this in detail in Chapters 6 and 7.

For now, let's look more at the basic benefits of a trust.

THE BENEFIT OF PLANNED CONTINUITY

The most basic reason for a family trust is to create continuity in your family after you are dead. You care about your family. You want them to experience continuity, not upheaval or disarray.

I once had a neighbor, Roger, who was also my client. I passed his house twice a day, once on the way to work and once on the way home. Being his attorney, I knew what he owned, how he owned it, what it was worth, why he owned it, and who he intended to benefit with it.[36] Roger and his wife had one

35 For an insightful rebuttal to the argument that trusts always create dependency, see James Grubman, Dennis Jaffe, and Kristin Keffeler, *Wealth 3.0: The Future of Family Wealth Advising* (Family Wealth Consulting 2023).

36 This name is fictitious, but this is a real example.

child, a young daughter. Enthusiastic about life, Roger delighted in behavior that would not occur to other people. Once, after he went through the drive-through with his daughter, he was concerned their food would get cold as he did other errands. He got out of the car, opened the hood, placed the styrofoam food container on the engine manifold to keep it warm, and continued on his way.

One Sunday morning, I drove past Roger's house to find a deputy sheriff's car in the driveway. I assumed Roger had had an exuberant party the night before. As soon as I arrived home, as my family and I sat down to eat breakfast, the phone rang. On the phone was the voice of a woman I did not know. She was the best friend of Roger's wife. "I'm sorry to bother you, but Roger died this morning when he was mowing his lawn. His tractor flipped over on him. Could you please get down here right away?"

I arrived at Roger's house after the sheriff but before the coroner.

Just an hour before Roger died, he had put his daughter on a school bus for a week-long summer camp outing. Roger's wife had to call the camp director and explain why their daughter needed to come home early.

Roger's primary ownership structure was a trust. The trust owned his business, his real estate ventures, his sizable life insurance policy, and his car collection. Because he had set up the ownership cohesively, and because he had created a trust that benefited his wife and daughter effectively, the trust became a source of continuity in Roger's household. His wife and daughter made their way through a terrible period. Despite their great sadness, they experienced relative stability.

THE BENEFIT OF INVESTING AS AN OWNER

A trust is a type of owner, and like all owners that invest in property, a trust invests. The trustee invests the trust's property so the property grows over time. The investments generate two types of value: principal, which is the investment's initial value plus growth on that value; and interest, which is the income (interest, dividends and so forth) the principal generates.

A trust's property is allocated across categories of risk and return, just as would happen if the investor were an individual person or a married couple. The asset allocation determines what types of investments the trust makes—for example, publicly-traded stocks, bonds, real estate, private equity. The mix depends on the trust's investment goals, time horizon, and willingness to take risks—the same as with an individual person.

With trusts, there is a further investment consideration—allocation to reflect risks across classes of beneficiaries and ages and stages of life of people in the family. For example, older beneficiaries who are more focused on interest income will look more to investments that generate income now, such as dividend-paying stocks. Younger beneficiaries who are more focused on the long-term strength of the trust's principal will look to investments that increase the principal. The trustee may find opportunities to make longer-range investments that benefit people who are beneficiaries farther in the future.

A trust's investing often has long-lasting consequences for a family. In the 1920s, Ben worked as a teller at the local bank. Like many people of that era, Ben did not attend college. He had some schooling, but at an early age he started working. Ben was notoriously frugal. He spent little, preferring instead to accumulate cash. When the United States fell into the Great Depression, stock prices for high quality, "blue chip" companies also fell. Bank stocks fell. At Ben's teller window, he watched formerly wealthy customers clamor for cash. Ben saw what was happening in the country. He began using his cash to buy blue chip stocks.

By the time the stock market recovered a decade later, Ben had made a lot of money. He placed his stock portfolio in a trust that benefited himself, his sister who became a widow at a young age, and her six children. He provided for the trust to run until the last of the six children died. The trust put them on much better financial footing. Meanwhile, Ben, sticking to his frugal ways, did not draw much for himself from the trust. Forty-five years later, Ben died in his late 90s. The last of his sister's children did not die until another 30 years after that. By then, the trust's investments had grown enough to pay substantial amounts to the remainder beneficiaries, Ben's sixteen nieces and nephews.

THE BENEFIT OF PROTECTING YOUR PROPERTY

One of the most important reasons to set up a trust is asset protection. The split ownership of a trust, where the beneficial owner (the beneficiary) is not the same as the legal owner (the trustee), deters creditors of beneficiaries. A creditor might try to seize money from a beneficiary—but the money's legal owner, the trustee, stands in the creditor's way.

Unfortunately, statistically today a person's biggest potential creditor is the person's spouse. This is why trusts are used to protect against the risk of a child divorcing.

Other asset protection risks are drug or alcohol misuse by beneficiaries, behavioral health problems experienced by beneficiaries, financial problems that extend even to bankruptcy, and general difficulties handling money. For all these risks, the trustee can be authorized to suspend distributions, so the money is not in the beneficiary's hand for a creditor to seize. The purpose is not to treat the beneficiary like a helpless baby but to protect the money for the beneficiary. After all, the grantor set up the trust to benefit the beneficiary, not creditors.

Protecting your property from creditors reinforces the decision of whom you want to benefit. Norbert, whose family wealth dated back six generations, made an investing mistake.

He invested in a re-insurance syndicate that incurred more insurance claims than it had money to pay the claims. Under the terms of Norbert's investment, if the syndicate came up short and needed cash, it was permitted to seize all of Norbert's property. Recognizing this risk when he made the investment, right away Norbert protected his daughter's house by owning the house in a trust to benefit her. Norbert named someone outside the family as trustee. Years later, when the syndicate collapsed, it sued all its investors, including Norbert. Unable to get control of the house, the syndicate sued Norbert, his daughter, and the trustee for fraud. Norbert's attorneys skillfully proved there was no fraud. Norbert's decision to benefit his daughter, and not the syndicate, was validated.

THE BENEFIT OF LOANS

Property that exits a trust need not exit permanently. A trust can be set up to make loans to the trust creator and loans to the beneficiaries. The trust creator might want to borrow from the trust to accomplish advanced estate planning. A beneficiary might want to borrow from the trust as a way to use the trust as a family bank.[37] Loans owed to the trust can be valuable assets of the trust. They can expand the trust's impact.

Roberta accumulated a fair amount of money from a suc-

37 For more on the family bank concept, see Chapter 7.

cessful career in the fragrance industry. She set up a trust for the specific purpose of loaning money to each of her four children, to enable them to buy houses when they reached age 30. She did not have the trust pay distributions to the children at that time. Instead, as each child turned 30, the trustee loaned the child money to finance a home purchase. Instead of paying a regular bank, the child paid the trustee on the home loan at a reduced interest rate. All four children paid their loans in full. Roberta received interest on her money. When Roberta died, the trustee distributed the paid-back loan proceeds, with the interest the trust had accumulated, to the children.

THE TAX BENEFITS

On this list, taxes come last. Tax reduction is a common reason to create a trust. In many cases it may be the top reason—as your professional advisor sees the world. From the *client's* vantage point, though, taxes alone are usually not the first concern. In my experience, if taxes alone are the client's first concern, the people involved in the trust will find the trust very unsatisfying.

But taxes are an important factor in designing a trust. As the saying goes, the federal estate tax is voluntary. It is possible to "disinherit" the IRS by designing trusts to defer and eliminate estate tax exposure. There are only three places you can go with your money: (1) taxes; (2) family and friends; (3) charity.

Every dollar a trust keeps from taxes is a dollar you can deploy to family, friends, or charity. It's a question of how you want to allocate your money.

Designing trusts to minimize taxes is a legitimate and important goal. The trick is to make sure the trust does not address taxes at the expense of ignoring the beneficiary, the family culture, and the trustee-beneficiary relationship. We'll talk more about this in Chapter 5.

THE OWNER

So there you have it. A trust is a type of owner. The ownership is split. There is the legal owner, and there is the beneficial owner. Behind each owner is a person.

Every trust begins and ends with a person. Every trust is set up by a person—someone who wants to benefit some other person. And every trust is owned by a person—someone responsible for owning it so it benefits a human being.

There's no good reason a trust can't be run to create this kind of benefit. The challenge is for the persons involved in a trust—the grantor, the trustee, and most of all the beneficiary—to integrate the trust into their lives. It's the Integrity Problem again. Strategizing to solve this problem is what we'll talk about next.

FOCUS QUESTIONS

1. Take a trust you are involved in. Based on the trust personnel lineup in this chapter, where are you in the lineup for this trust?

2. Who are all the people this trust benefits?

3. Is this trust run with the beneficiaries at the center? If not, what needs to happen for them to be at the center?

4. How are the people associated with this trust turning out? Is the trust helping them or damaging them? Why?

5. What are the greatest benefits this trust could provide its beneficiaries? What needs to happen to maximize these benefits?

CHAPTER FIVE

TRUSTS AND THE STRATEGY OF OWNERSHIP

"Good or bad, we must make the portage."

—**MERIWETHER LEWIS, THE CORPS OF DISCOVERY, JUNE 16, 1805**

The Lewis and Clark expedition is more than a story. It's a true American epic.

From 1804 to 1806, acting under commission of President Thomas Jefferson, Meriwether Lewis and William Clark led a team of 33 people, the "Corps of Discovery," to learn about the western United States and find an inland waterway passage to the Pacific Ocean. Traveling up the Missouri River from St. Louis, they boated smaller rivers across North Dakota, Montana, and Idaho, eventually traversing the Columbia River down through Oregon to the Pacific. The Corps displayed extraordinary focus and stamina, contending with grizzly bears, deluges, wolves, hail, rattlesnakes, mosquitos, grave illnesses, days without food, and in Lewis's case, being accidentally shot.

Remarkably, none of the group died.[38]

Good strategic decisions were critical to the expedition's success. One of the most important decisions took place on the upper Missouri River in Montana, where the group discovered the Great Falls of the Missouri. The roaring water and clouds of spray marked the dramatic entrance to the Rocky Mountains. Though the cascades and rapids in the river posed a problem, the real problem was the need to portage everything—get out of the boats and move the boats, the equipment, the supplies, and the horses—around the falls. Portaging the Great Falls involved an eighteen-mile detour that took an entire month.[39]

With the group's native guide, Sacagawea, incapacitated due to illness, Meriwether Lewis dispatched two teams of scouts—one to search each side of the river for an optimal place to portage. Eventually the scouts returned to Lewis with "a very unfavorable report": the ravines were so steep that a portage was inadvisable.[40] Getting out of the boats and moving all the personnel, equipment and animals overland was very dangerous.

Sizing up the situation, Lewis rendered a decision—perhaps the single most important of the trip so far—to proceed anyway.

---

38 Gary Moulton, ed., *The Lewis and Clark Journals: An American Epic of Discovery*, by Meriwether Lewis, William Clark, and the Corps of Discovery (University of Nebraska Press 2003).

39 Id., p. xxix.

40 Id., p. 135.

He said simply, "Good or bad, we must make the portage."[41]

Lewis's decision parallels the decisions a family owner must make about ownership in trust. Any good decision emerges from strategy, and strategy is about making specific choices. Strategy is choice.[42] Only through making and acting on choices can you succeed. Tough choices force your hand and confine you, yet these very choices free you to focus.[43]

With family trusts, as with rivers, sometimes a placid, direct trip is not possible. Sometimes you have to get out, put your belongings on your back, and walk. Especially when you are entering new country, where others never have been, you do not know how the walk will unfold. Yet you do not walk alone, and you glimpse enough of a path to sense how the venture could turn out quite well.[44]

In fact, the act of getting out, moving the boat, and walking is not a setback. It's a chance to re-assess the terrain accurately, so that when you put the boat back in the water, the rest of your journey is better, not worse. You are not defeated. You're simply being realistic.

The first step is to identify the barriers around which you must maneuver.

41 Id., p. 135.

42 A.G. Lafley and Roger L. Martin, *Playing To Win: How Strategy Really Works* (Harvard Business Review Press 2013), pp. 2-5, 14-34.

43 Id., p. 5.

44 Moulton, pp. xxvi, 92-93.

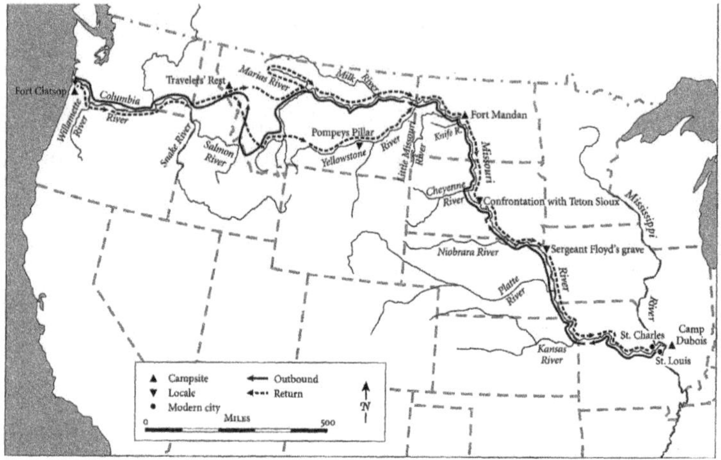

A map of the Lewis and Clark Expedition adapted from their journals.[45] Every journey takes place in a real-world, physical location—it's important to envisage your journey in as real and tangible terms as these explorers' trek across the continent.

PORTAGING AROUND HUMAN IMPERFECTION

Coming to terms with ownership in family trusts requires portaging around three major obstacles.

FEAR

The first is fear—the risk of being seen as dependent on the trust. You have met people called "trust fund babies," and you

45 Gary Moulton, ed., *The Lewis and Clark Journals: An American Epic of Discovery*, by Meriwether Lewis, William Clark, and the Corps of Discovery (University of Nebraska Press 2003).

know you don't want to be like them. More precisely, you don't want to be *looked upon* as being like them.

Here's an example of what you don't want – and why fear is a real obstacle.

A colleague of mine, Meghan, graduated from a high-caliber east coast university. Meghan was able to afford the school's high tuition only by a combination of merit scholarships and student loans. Meghan's roommate, by contrast, had no such concerns. The roommate's family had quite a bit of money. As a first-year college student, the roommate had multiple credit cards—one for clothing, one for food and entertainment, and one for travel. If she wanted a new outfit, she charged the clothing card. If she wanted to go out and socialize, she charged the entertainment card. If she wanted to go away for the weekend, she charged the travel card.

When on occasion Meghan had to decline plans like going to the movies or on Spring Break trips for lack of money, the roommate would look at her quizzically and say, "Just use your credit card." The roommate had trouble understanding why Meghan had no credit cards at all.

The roommate was not especially studious, preferring to watch tv in the dorm room while Meghan was in class. When Meghan asked her what she did during the summer, the roommate answered in terms of activities, such as watching tv or sitting by the pool, and not in terms of working in a job, cleaning the house, planning a career, or the like. Eventually, the roommate explained that cash came to her from a family trust, so performing work in exchange for pay was not on her radar. In fact, she didn't seem to understand what paid employment was. When she wanted Meghan to come along for social activities but Meghan's part-time job waiting tables—which paid all her living expenses—had her scheduled for work shifts, the roommate would say, "Just tell them you're not coming in this week," and then be confused at Meghan's exasperation.

This roommate was living in an unreal world that most of her peers did not inhabit. She had no idea how to relate to or navigate life outside her cosseted trust bubble. She had a serious handicap and did not know it. The trust had cut her off from any experience of scarcity—and genuine friendship.

No one wants to be that roommate (and even more, no parents want their child to be that roommate). No one even wants to be seen as coming across like her. No one wants to be perceived as cut off from ordinary human relationships due to money flowing from a trust. Being cut off is painful. No one wishes to be resented, and certainly not resented for clinging to dependency.

ANXIETY

The second risk is anxiety—the uneasy feeling that you simply will not be able to understand the trust agreement and how the trust works. If asked, most people voice deep frustration at being unable to understand what a trust agreement says. No one buys a car expecting to have no idea how to drive it. Many car manufacturers make the car intuitive enough that the driver does not need to read the owner's manual. Honda is the preeminent example. When you sit in the driver's seat of a Honda, the dashboard controls are so intuitive you can figure them out within a few minutes. Very few trust agreements are this intuitive.

As we saw in Chapter 4, trusts involve split ownership. There is the legal owner, and there are the beneficial owners. With a car, there is a driver who operates the controls and a passenger who does not. With a trust, by contrast, both the driver and the passenger are owners. Even the passenger has a certain amount of control. Beneficiaries of a trust are no different than passengers in a car: they become upset at not being able to understand what a "car" is, much less how the controls work and which controls they operate. This frustration creates anxiety. Most people wouldn't ride in a machine hurtling along at nearly 100 miles per hour without having a basic idea of what to expect. Yet trust beneficiaries are asked to do this every day.

IMMOBILITY

The third risk is immobility—the inability to take action due to an overall dread of failure. This risk may seem counterintuitive to you. Why, you ask, if a person has access to ample money in a trust, does the person feel unable to move? Shouldn't the money free up the person? Isn't that the very point of the money?

The answer is that the very existence of the money creates for the beneficiary the daunting prospect of being seen as not using the money effectively. No beneficiary wants to be a failed beneficiary. Every beneficiary wants to do right by the money. If you are the beneficiary, you want to show you have used the money well and not wasted it. Yet if you, the beneficiary, don't feel you are truly free to use the money, you can't start to use it. You can't run a race if you can't even get out of the starting gate.

The adventurer confronting a family trust must portage around all three of these barriers lying across the path.

As Meriwether Lewis said, the portage is not optional. You have to do it. Doing it is the only way forward.

STEPS OF THE PORTAGE

If making a portage is something you must do, how do you make the portage happen? What steps should you follow?

Your overall goal should be to put the people involved in the trust, and especially the beneficiaries, at the center. The Corps of Discovery succeeded because it kept all of the 33 people at the center. The Corps did not lose one person during the entire 28 months of the journey.

Your trust should have this same goal: keep the people at the center, and lose no one.

How do you make this happen? If strategy is about choice, how do you choose well?

This chapter suggests four steps:

1. Discover the origins of the trust. Find out everything you can about why the trust was created.
2. Apply your attention to understanding the trust. Read the trust agreement, and talk to the trustee.
3. Apply the Three-Circle Model to see where you stand, both now and in the future.
4. Become a Self-Governing Beneficiary®.[46]

Let's look at each of these steps in turn.

STEP 1: DISCOVER THE ORIGINS

The Lewis and Clark expedition was a search for origins. Thomas Jefferson wanted the Corps of Discovery to find out how the western part of the United States came to be. Lewis and Clark knew the Missouri River ended in St. Louis, but where did the Missouri River start? What were the various tribes of Native Americans like? What were their customs? What did the

46 "Self-Governing Beneficiary" is a registered trademark of The Family Enterprise Office, LLC.

wildlife look like, and how much wildlife was there? What did the Rocky Mountains look like? Where did the Columbia River begin? It ended at the Pacific Ocean, but where did it begin? All these questions pertained to how things originated. The Corps was on a search for beginnings.

Trusts are like this. Everyone who looks at a trust agreement should want to know the trust's origins. Why did the grantor decide to create a trust? Why did the grantor decide to benefit this particular beneficiary? How long did the grantor spend thinking about creating a trust? What thoughts went through the grantor's mind during the whole process?

Trust beneficiaries especially want to know the origins. Beneficiaries long to know why someone decided to benefit them. They're curious. It's a bit like returning to the city where you were born, or driving past your old house or your old school. Even more, it's like taking in the place where your parents or grandparents were born, or where they died. The place is a tie to you, and you appreciate it by seeing it, learning about it, talking about it. You ask yourself, how did this particular past originate? How did it come to form who I am now and what I do today?

This is why trusts where the grantor is alive offer a huge advantage over trusts where the grantor is deceased. A beneficiary can sit in a chair, read the trust agreement, and learn some of the grantor's thinking about the trust. But reading the trust agreement is not as informative, and certainly not as satisfying, as having an in-person conversation with the grantor about the grantor's thinking. As we saw in Chapter 4, a trust is a relationship of persons.[47] The best way to have a relationship with someone is through in-person conversation.

THINKING LIKE AN OWNER

Talking to a live grantor improves the beneficiary's ability to develop an ownership mindset toward the trust. Some grantors create trusts that are quite open-ended. They do not say much of anything about how the beneficiary might succeed with the money in the trust. Other grantors create trusts that are archly prescriptive. They specify exactly what the beneficiary shall do, when the beneficiary shall do it, and how the beneficiary shall not deviate from the path the grantor has set. With either type of trust, when you ask the grantor how the beneficiary should turn out, almost always the grantor will say the beneficiary should think like an owner. Now, the grantor may have trouble turning over enough control for this actually to happen. But an ownership mindset is what the grantor desires for the beneficiary.

An ownership mindset is also what most beneficiaries want. To acquire one, they must portage about the obstacles of fear, anxiety, and immobility. As they handle the obstacles, they think more like an owner.

47 Scott and Ascher on Trusts, 6th ed., Chapter 2.1.3.

In-person conversations between grantor and beneficiary are the best way for a beneficiary to think like an owner within a trust. When the grantor is still alive, this advantage is available. Take advantage of it. Don't wait.

LEARNING THE ORIGINS INDIRECTLY

What do you do when the grantor is deceased? How do you learn about the trust's origins in that case? The trust agreement is available to you, and you should make sure to read it. You also can consult people who knew what the grantor had in mind—a family member, a friend of the grantor, or a professional advisor of the grantor (lawyer, accountant, investment advisor). Make sure you seek out those people who are unconflicted enough to give you an accurate explanation.

Depending on who the trustee is, you may obtain considerable insight into the grantor's thinking by talking with the trustee. Generally, the closer the relationship the trustee had with the grantor, the more you will uncover the grantor's thinking by asking the trustee.

Last, if the grantor wrote down anything, such as letters or notes to you, letters to other family members, instructions to professional advisors, or instructions to the trustee, you should ask to read them. They will affect how you develop an ownership mindset—a frame of mind the grantor desired you to acquire.

STEP 2: APPLY YOUR ATTENTION AS A BENEFICIARY

In making the journey to understand your trust, you, the beneficiary, have one quality more valuable than any others. This quality is your attention.

Some people say time is your most valuable resource, but this isn't quite right. Your most valuable resource is your attention. Your attention is property you own.[48] In fact, it's probably the most valuable property you own. Focusing your attention develops your ownership of this irreplaceable property that exists inside you, the beneficiary.[49]

The first way to use your attention is to read and learn the trust agreement. The second way is to have in-person conversations with the grantor, if they are alive. The third way is to have in-person conversations with the trustee.

That's right, the trustee needs to be an object of your attention. Rather than using your attention to watch television or scroll on your phone, apply your attention to talking to the trustee. You will learn something.

Beneficiaries usually find talking to trustees uncomfortable. Many beneficiaries look upon the trust as an arranged

48 Dan Sullivan, *Your Attention: Your Property* (The Strategic Coach, Inc. 2021), p. 35.

49 Concerning the fragmentation of a person's attention due to excessive use of the Internet and especially cell phones, see Haidt, *The Anxious Generation*, pp. 113-141.

marriage. The beneficiaries see the trustee as the person in this marriage who holds the keys to the kingdom. The shortcomings of both trustee and beneficiary compound this problem. Some trustees are bureaucratic and condescending, which of course makes the beneficiaries resentful and distrusting. Beneficiaries, for their part, often feel unworthy of the gift the grantor made them in the trust, which makes the beneficiaries reticent. Both parties to the conversation—both trustee and beneficiary—can strengthen the relationship by improving their communication with each other.

If you are a beneficiary, the best step you can take is to ask the trustee questions. Don't wait for the trustee to get in touch with you. In this particular case, waiting is not useful. Draw up your list of questions, and go talk to the trustee. Your questions don't need to be complicated. They just need to be designed to get answers. You could use questions like these:

1. Why did you, the trustee, sign up for this job? What do you like best about it? What do you dislike about it?
2. What are you, the trustee, responsible for? What are you not responsible for?
3. When people say you, the trustee, are a "fiduciary," what do they mean? What do you mean?
4. What am I, the beneficiary, responsible for? What am I not responsible for?
5. How would you, the trustee, like to get to know me, the

beneficiary? How can I help you get to know me?

6. What do I, the beneficiary, need to know about the financial and investing concepts involved in trusts?
7. What do you, the trustee, think I need in order to supplement my education about trusts? How should I go about learning more?
8. How are you, the trustee, paid? What factors determine whether your pay increases? Does your pay ever decrease?

For more questions to give substance to the trustee-beneficiary relationship, see the Focus Questions at the end of this chapter.

STEP 3: APPLY THE THREE-CIRCLE MODEL

In Chapter 3, we looked at the Three-Circle Model. Take a look at the following Enhanced Three Circle Model Diagram; you will notice there is no circle marked "trusts." There is a circle for Owners. There is a circle for Family. There is a circle for Management. But there is no circle for trusts.

Situating a trust on the Three-Circle Model is tricky. Where should a trust go?

Here's the diagram again, this time with the roles of trustee and beneficiary of an enterprise-owning trust imposed on it.

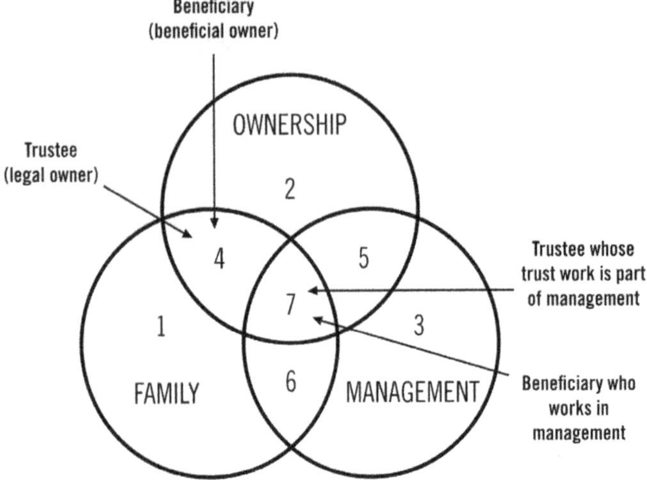

As we saw in Chapter 4, the trustee, and not any one beneficiary, is the legal owner of a trust. The trustee is legally responsible for the trust's property. Yet a beneficiary is also an owner of a trust. A beneficiary is a beneficial owner.

Because both trustee and beneficiary are owners of the trust, you can make a good case that both of them should be depicted on the Three-Circle Model. But where?

Both of them should go in the circle where Ownership and Family overlap (segment 4 on the Model). Identifying them separately, as trustee and beneficiary, illustrates the point that each is a type of owner.

Now, you could argue that since the trust benefits the grantor's family, the beneficiary also should simply go in the circle for Family, without regard to Ownership (segment 1 on the Model). After all, the beneficiary is a member of the family. However, if you are trying to pinpoint who the owners of the enterprise are, you will want to distinguish between being a member of the family and being an *owner* of an entity, a trust, that affects the family's activities. For this reason, we list the beneficiary in segment 4, not segment 1, on the Model. The point is not simply that the beneficiary is part of the family; the point is that among members of the family, the beneficiary is an owner.

Similarly, if the trustee is an individual who is a member of the family, he or she goes in segment 4 on the Model, to illustrate that although he or she is a family member, he or she has fiduciary duties as the legal owner of a trust that benefits the family.

What if either the trustee or the beneficiary, or both of them, work as management-level employees of a family enterprise that the diagram depicts? In that case, you might place them in the middle of the Model, in segment 7, to show they are family members, they work for the enterprise, and they are involved in management.

Two further points arise here. First, if you are the trustee in segment 7, not only are you engaged in the work of being a trustee, but in addition you are engaged in the work of managing the enterprise. You might even be the president of the enterprise. Second, if you are wearing the hats of both trustee and manager, you owe two sets of duties to two groups of people, which exposes you to conflicts of interest. On the one hand, as manager you owe corporate officer duties to the enterprise itself. On the other hand, as trustee you also owe the fiduciary duties of trustee to beneficial owners of the enterprise. Sorting out these potential conflicts can be tricky. You as trustee must be careful, and the beneficiaries must realize you need to be careful.

THE THREE-CIRCLE MODEL AND YOUR FUTURE

If instead you are the beneficiary, you can use the Three-Circle Model to envision and plan for your future. Using the model, you can see the circles to which you and others in your family might move. When you use the model this way, you see that each person actually has a limited number of places to which they can move.

For example, if your family's policy is not to offer ownership to a member of management, a person in the Management circle will never end up in the Owner circle. A person in your family who does not want to work for the enterprise will never occupy the CEO slot in the middle of the circles—not because the person isn't qualified, but because the person doesn't want to work there. A family member who takes over as trustee will move to the Owner circle as legal owner, but not to the Management circle (unless he or she also works for the enterprise). And so on.

Using the model, you can see where your trustee-beneficiary relationship could become vulnerable in the future. For example, if upon the death of the current trustee who is an individual in the family, the trust calls for a trustee that is a corporation, and the individual is older and in declining health, you can see that the composition of the Owner circle is going to change once the corporate trustee gets involved. This kind of change could be significant. The corporate trustee's ways of working may not match how the other owners operate.

Or to take another example: if a current beneficiary in the Family circle is in declining health, the other remainder beneficiaries, who also are in the Family circle, will need to gain more knowledge about how the trust works. They will need to step toward a closer relationship with the trustee.

Remember, a trust is a relationship of persons. The Three-Circle Model is a useful way to see how this relationship unfolds over time in the environment of ownership in your family.

To help you adjust to thinking in terms of the Three-Circle Model, we've placed a blank Model diagram in the back of this book. Use it whenever you feel stuck.

STEP 4: BECOME A SELF-GOVERNING BENEFICIARY®

The Lewis and Clark expedition succeeded for many reasons, but the fundamental reason was mindset. The Corps of

Discovery, all 33 people, had the mindset to make the venture a success.

Early on, the Corps traveled through land that had been explored already. But eventually, in North Dakota, the Corps crossed into country where no one had ever been, save Native Americans and a handful of traders. From western North Dakota to the Pacific Ocean was all new. As Meriwether Lewis wrote, "We were now about to penetrate a country at least two thousand miles in width . . . the good or evil it had in store for us was for experiment yet to determine. . . ."[50]

The group was venturing into the unknown.

Rather than being afraid, Lewis found this moment exciting. In his notes he explained:

> Entertaining, as I do, the most confident hope of succeeding in [this] voyage . . . I could but esteem this moment of my departure as among the most happy of my life. The party are in excellent health and spirits, zealously attached to the enterprise, and anxious to proceed; not a whisper or murmur of discontent to be heard among them, but all act in unison, and with the most perfect harmony.[51]

Think about this. Rather than being fearful or worried,

---

50 Moulton, pp. 92-93.

51 Moulton, p. 93.

Lewis considered this first step into the unknown the happiest moment of his life. He also described three key attributes of his co-venturers: confidence, zealous attachment to the enterprise, and harmony.

These three attributes—confidence, attachment, harmony—are the same ones families seek in their co-ownership. You yourself seek them. That's why you're reading this book.

Lewis shows you how a beneficiary of a trust can experience hope similar to what the Corps of Discovery experienced. A beneficiary is on a journey of discovery, into the unknown land of trusts. There is no reason a beneficiary cannot be successful on this journey. Often, the missing ingredient is mindset.

To have an optimal trustee-beneficiary relationship, and to get the most out of a trust, you should aspire to be a Self-Governing Beneficiary®.[52] A Self-Governing Beneficiary is a trust beneficiary who has the capability of being informed, mature, and self-possessed enough to, with the right help, someday be their own trustee if the current trustee could not serve or all the trust assets were distributed.

Note this definition. A Self-Governing Beneficiary might start out uninformed, immature, and not self-possessed. But over time, the Self-Governing Beneficiary becomes informed enough, mature enough, and self-possessed enough to serve as trustee. Let's suppose you are the beneficiary. Being a Self-Gov-

52 "Self-Governing Beneficiary" is a registered trademark of The Family Enterprise Office, LLC.

erning Beneficiary does not mean you will ever actually be trustee. It simply means that you acquire the qualities and skills necessary to be capable of serving. It means you are on the ball enough that if you were called upon to step in and serve, you could.

What mindsets are useful for being a Self-Governing Beneficiary? Here are some:

1. Humble Learner: You want to learn what the trust can do for you, and most of all you want to learn how to be a good beneficiary.
2. Hard Worker: You work hard because your work reflects your desire to be a conscientious steward of the trust.
3. Asset Maximizer: You look at what the money in the trust can do, not just how much is there.
4. Open to Gifts: You accept the challenge that the trust calls you to be a good receiver, not just a good giver, of gifts.
5. Intergenerational Thinker: You treat the money in the trust as a very important advantage for multiple generations of your family.
6. Collaborator: You work toward a collaborative relationship with your trustee and advisors, to use the trust's assets to help you flourish as a person.
7. Owner: You want to appreciate the trust as an owner,

not just a legal structure, because you see it as central to your family's ownership of important assets.

8. Self-Governing: You aspire to govern yourself, be in charge of your own situation with appropriate guidance, and to be able to take over as trustee if need be.

On the following pages is a scorecard for you to measure yourself based on these mindsets. Here's how the scorecard works. In the far left column are the mindsets. For each mindset there is a numerical range, numbered from 1 to 12 (left to right), spread over the next four columns. For each mindset, give yourself a number that fits where you fall on the range. For example, if you feel you are about a 5, assign yourself the number five. Write that number in the far right column labeled "Score Now." This number represents how you feel you rate right now.

After giving yourself a "Score Now" for each mindset, total your "Score Now" numbers and enter their total at the bottom of the scorecard. This is your "Score Now" total.

Then go back and score yourself with the number you would *like* to attain for each mindset in the next 12 months. This is your "Score Next" number for that mindset. For example, if you could like to improve from 5 to 10, assign yourself the number 10 in the far right column labeled "Score Next".

After giving yourself a "Score Next" for each mindset, total your "Score Next" numbers and enter their total at the bottom of the scorecard. This is your "Score Next" total.

Now you have an idea of how you want to progress toward being a Self-Governing Beneficiary. You have a clearer idea of what you want, what you don't want, and how you might get there.

Once you start thinking in terms of being a Self-Governing Beneficiary, you'll probably want to update your Scorecard periodically. You can find a downloadable blank scorecard at takeownershipofwhatyouown.com for this purpose.[53]

Mindsets	1 to 3	4 to 6	7 to 9	10 to 12	Score Now	Score Next
1. Humble Learner	You don't understand how people less knowledgeable than you achieve smooth results with their trusts.	You've tried to learn how your trust works, but you just can't seem to get it.	You read everything the trustee sends you, and you still don't feel in command of the subject matter.	You want to learn what the trust can do for you, and most of all you want to learn how to be a good beneficiary.		
2. Hard Worker	You don't work at anything because the trust has robbed you of all incentive for work.	You would like to work hard at something for yourself, but the trust weighs on you and holds you back.	You've worked at what was expected of you, and now it's time to kick back and enjoy the trust distributions.	You work hard because your work reflects your desire to be a conscientious steward of the trust.		

53 The Self-Governing Beneficiary Mindset Scorecard is subject to copyright of The Family Enterprise Office, LLC.

3. Asset Maximizer	You don't have much to show for the money the trust makes available to you.	You don't understand why there hasn't been more growth in the trust assets and in the things you have spent trust distributions on.	You have more to show for the trust and your expenditures than most other people in your situation.	You look at what the money from the trust can do, not just how much is there.		
4. Open to Gifts	You feel insignificant and unworthy next to the gift that the money in this trust represents.	You've tried to feel and show gratitude about the trust, but every time you feel like the trust controls you.	You see the money in the trust as a gift to you, and you're content not to ponder the reasons for the gift.	You accept the challenge that the trust calls you to be a good receiver, not just a good giver of gifts.		
5. Intergenerational Thinker	Your primary focus is what the money can do for you while you're alive. Those after you can figure it out for themselves.	You wonder how the trust is supposed to connect you to those after you, and you struggle to grasp a clear connection.	You see the trust as a great resource for multiple generations, and you realize someone in the family should pay more attention to it.	You treat the money in the trust as a very important advantage for multiple generations of your family.		

6. Collaborative	Your trustee is a small-minded bureaucrat who always manages to make you feel like a loser.	You often feel like you and your trustee work against each other instead of together.	You and you trustee have an acceptable working relationship, given the circumstances.	You work toward a collaborative relationship with your trustee and advisors, to use the trust's assets to help you flourish.		
7. Trusts as Owners	All your family's advisors treat you like the money in the trust is a reflection solely of the person who set it up.	You're tired of being treated like someone who doesn't have a real ownership stake in the trust.	You feel certain you've learned as much as you need to about how the trust owns things.	You want to appreciate the trust as an owner, not just a legal structure, because you see it as central to your family's ownership of important assets.		
8. Self-Governing	You feel dependent on the trust, which makes you resentful.	You want to be more in charge of how the trust supports a bigger future for you, and you don't know how.	You're satisfied that you've avoided becoming too dependent on the trust.	You aspire to govern yourself, to be in charge of your own situation with appropriate guidance, and to be able to take over as a trustee if need be.		
TOTALS						

THE PATIENCE OF PORTAGING

As you size up your mindsets as a beneficiary, realize that no matter how long the trust has existed or how many beneficiaries have preceded you, you are doing something *new*. Maybe you never have been a beneficiary before. Maybe you never have been involved in a trust that owns this kind of asset. Maybe you are entering a new era of your life. Maybe you have been a beneficiary for years but never a Self-Governing Beneficiary. Even if the trust or the asset has existed for many years, it is somehow new to you. You are embarking on a new venture, and you need to be patient with yourself.

To be successful, your venture, like the Corps of Discovery, must place the people at the center. The primary reason people become frustrated with trusts is that they view a trust not as a relationship but a piece of machinery, not an owner but a payment system. You correct these misperceptions by putting the people—the grantor, the trustee, the beneficiaries, and everyone else involved—at the center and not the periphery. Standing on the periphery is lonely. Beneficiaries, especially, need to be at the center. The trust exists for the people it is intended to benefit, not the other way around.

To see how a trust beneficiary can develop the mindsets to embark on the venture, make the necessary portages, and become a Self-Governing Beneficiary, we turn now to the question of Unique Ability.

FOCUS QUESTIONS

1. Take a family trust you are involved in. When it comes to this trust, how have you experienced the obstacles of fear, anxiety, and immobility?

2. What can you do to discover the origins of this trust?

3. What questions do you most want to ask the trustee of this trust? (If you are the trustee, what questions do you most want to discuss with the beneficiaries?)

4. Looking again at the Three-Circle Model, where does your role in the trust place you on the Model? Where will you likely be on the Model 10 years from now?

5. Please fill out the Mindset Scorecard for a Self-Governing Beneficiary. (You can download a blank Mindset Scorecard at takeownershipofwhatyouown.com.) Which aspects of a Self-Governing Beneficiary do you most need to work on over the next 18 months?

CHAPTER SIX

OWNING YOUR UNIQUENESS

"The grand invitation is to embrace the reality of your life and figure out what to do with it."

—MICHAEL ERWIN AND RAYMOND KETHLEDGE, LEAD YOURSELF FIRST

Once, I was standing in the lobby of a restaurant at lunch time, waiting to be called to my table, when I witnessed a revealing interaction.

Across the lobby stood a young man and his business partner. The young man was the son of a CEO of an innovative, fast-growing, publicly traded company. The father had driven the company to the front ranks of American business. He owned many shares of the company's stock.

The CEO's son stood in the restaurant lobby quietly talking with his business partner. Suddenly, in walked a loud-talking banker who asked the son's name, and upon hearing it, asked him if his father was the prominent CEO.

When the son said yes, the banker shouted, "Wow! Aren't you lucky!"—implying that the son would never need to work for a living.

The son's business partner's face darkened, and he retorted quickly, "No, his dad's the lucky one—lucky to have a son like this."

How children differentiate themselves from their parents is a challenge and a mystery. It's a challenge because it's universal. It's something all children and most parents want. Whether the child is a self-driven person who creates something from nothing, or whether the child creates a life using what the parents originated, all children want to have their own lives.

Differentiation is also a mystery because there is no set program for whether, how, and when it happens. It is not guaranteed to occur. You can't buy a product to bring it about. It's not like a box cake mix. Experts have written all kinds of books about how children differentiate, and they don't agree on how the process unfolds. Some children differentiate from their parents in stunningly impressive ways. Other children struggle their whole lives to make any progress.

The issue is more challenging when a trust is involved. A common complaint of parents who create trusts is that their children do not handle money well. The parents fear the children will become pathetically dependent on the trust. These same parents almost never examine their own lives and consider how they themselves have and have not used money well.

They allow their own fear to consume the time they could apply toward useful self-reflection. You wonder whether the parents fear discovering that they themselves are impermanent.[54]

Regardless of what problems might be hobbling the parents, recall from Chapter 3 that individuation is the cure for entitlement.[55] A child who becomes his or her own person is less likely to find entitlement appealing. Such a child is more likely to see that entitlement erodes a person's sense of self-worth.

Ownership requires responsibility, accountability, and a confidence of bearing that defines the decisions and actions of the owner. These traits are typically present in most children, but while parents are still involved in the trust, children may find it difficult to step fully into these traits. They are intimidated and accustomed to the parent-child relationship, to the detriment of stepping into ownership.

So far in this book, we have looked at how trusts can support family members who desire to become their own persons instead of becoming entitled. In Chapters 4 and 5, we considered how trusts can support this process. Now, in this chapter and Chapter 7, I present two concepts that strengthen a family trust by accelerating and deepening a child's differentiation from parents and individuation into being his or her own person.

Neither concept is original to me. The first one, Unique

---

54 Scott, *Fierce Conversations*, p. 76.

55 Hughes, *Complete Family Wealth*, p. 43.

Ability, comes from the mind of Dan Sullivan, founder of the Strategic Coach program for entrepreneurs. We'll look at Unique Ability in this chapter. Then, in Chapter 7, we'll look at the second concept, Entrepreneurial Stewardship, which comes from Stuart Lucas, who teaches a course on intergenerational family investing at the University of Chicago.[56] We'll see how these two concepts, which come from two different worlds, reinforce each other, and how applying them to a family trust can make both concepts concrete for your family. In the process, you will see how a trust is a type of owner that offers unique value to those whom it is intended to benefit.

Let's turn now to the concept of Unique Ability.

UNIQUE ABILITY

Each person is unique. In families, children may resemble their parents in personality and temperament as much as appearance. But every child is his or her own person. Each child is like the parents somehow, yet distinct. When you call the parent's phone, the child may answer and sound just like the parent. Yet you know the child is not the parent. The child is

56 Neither concept is original to me. The credit for the concept of Unique Ability goes to Dan Sullivan, founder of The Strategic Coach program. The credit for the concept of Entrepreneurial Stewardship goes to Stuart Lucas and his course in Private Wealth Management at the University of Chicago Booth School of Business.

someone entirely new. In fact, not one person in all of human history has been exactly like this child. When a child comes on the scene, something new for all time is happening.

Being unique, each person has a unique composite of abilities, or if you like, talents. This composite of abilities or talents resides in the essence of the person. To be clear: the abilities are not the same as the person's personality. I am not proposing that what a person is able to do is the same as who a person is. Neither an infant nor an elderly person is able to do certain things that an adult age 35 is able to do. The infant is not less a person. Nor is the elderly person less a person. Instead, I am proposing that the person's abilities, inherent in him or her, get at the essence of that person. The person's abilities are central to who that person is and what makes him or her distinct. Each one of these abilities, or talents, comprises a composite "Unique Ability" of the person.[57]

Every Unique Ability of a person involves four characteristics.[58]

First, the Unique Ability involves superior skill. The person has a way of doing something that stands out. They have an ability that other people notice and value.

Second, the Unique Ability involves passion. The person

57 The Strategic Coach program uses the term "Unique Ability" in the singular, to connote the aggregate set of unique talents of a person. However, your Unique Ability likely consists of many such individual talents. In this book, the plural sense of the term may be useful to you when the context fits.

58 Catherine Nomura, Julia Waller and Shannon Waller, *Unique Ability 2.0 Discovery*, p. 20 (The Strategic Coach, Inc. 2015).

has a drive to use the ability as much as possible—because using it activates who the person truly is.

Third, the Unique Ability involves energy. It's invigorating. Using the ability creates vitality, both for the person and those who experience him or her.

Fourth, the Unique Ability involves never-ending improvement. Unique Ability has a certain infinite quality to it. When the person uses the ability, the person gets better and better at it. While using the ability, the person never runs out of possibilities to grow.[59]

What does Unique Ability look like in real life? Here are three examples:

PATRICK

My friend Patrick has the Unique Ability of being a strategist. He is a superior strategist, able to determine easily and quickly what the key decisions are, which factors comprise those decisions, and what needs to be done to execute the decisions. He approaches strategic decisions with vigor and enthusiasm. Through his incisive use of strategy, he has become an innovator in his field, having created a large professional services business from scratch.

59 Id., pp., 24, 46.

LAURA

Laura has cerebral palsy. She experiences life from the seat of a motorized wheelchair. She can walk, but not well and not far. She has trouble speaking. Using the muscles in her mouth to form words is hard for her. Yet Laura has the Unique Ability of organizing information. She has a photographic memory. She has tremendous facility for the written word—studying it, remembering it, recording it, communicating it in writing. She applies her Unique Ability by working as a research librarian at a public university.

PAUL

My friend Paul has the Unique Ability of navigating objections to accomplish a goal. The second-generation president of a large family-owned company, Paul has tremendous patience in leading a group of people toward a decision. He is almost supernaturally calm. He systematically lays out what needs to be accomplished in a meeting. He assigns the meeting tasks to the right people. In meetings, he fields objections without getting upset or taking criticism personally. When someone objects, he finds a way forward. By using his Unique Ability, he has helped the company become many times more valuable than when he began as president.

UNIQUE ABILITY VERSUS EXCELLENCE

To appreciate just how important Unique Ability is to your life, and especially to your life as a co-owner of assets with your family, you must bear in mind three other points about how Unique Ability works.

First, your Unique Ability may make a big impression on other people and no impression on you. When you use your Unique Ability, you make what you do look easy. What feels natural and effortless to you may come across as brilliant and rare to others. Because you are situated so close to your own Unique Ability, you may have trouble appreciating your own uniqueness.[60] Don't be fooled. You do have Unique Ability, and you do use it.

Second, Unique Ability lies beyond excellence. Your Unique Ability is not the same as activities you perform excellently. Unique Ability activities are ones you simply love to engage in. You do them exceedingly well. They are your favorite ways to spend your time. You could do them all day long and not become tired. You would desire and enjoy them even if no one paid you to perform them.[61]

You also have activities at which you are excellent. You have superior ability to do them, and you find accomplishing them rewarding. People come to you for them, due to your reputation for doing them well. But—and this is the key difference—you

60 Id., p. 31.

61 Id., pp. 47-48.

do not have the passion for them that you do for your Unique Ability activities.[62] These "excellent activities" do not activate you—make you feel fully alive—as your Unique Ability activities do. Over time, they may even make you feel incomplete.

Third, once you know for sure what your Unique Ability is, you will want to use it to filter how you spend your time and allocate your attention. You will want to build your schedule with them at the center. Life is too short not to rivet your attention on your Unique Ability and maximize your use of it.

What do the people who know you best see as your Unique Ability? Have you asked them?[63]

UNIQUE ABILITY AND CO-OWNERSHIP

Having uncovered the secret of Unique Ability, we turn now to co-ownership of family assets. What does your Unique Ability have to do with your life as a co-owner? Quite a bit, it turns out. At the beginning of this book, we considered how family owners often feel stuck. They find coming to terms with what they own immensely challenging. Integrating what they own and who they are is a genuine problem. We've called this the Integrity Problem. Often they doubt themselves. Self-doubt drives them to want to know why they were made owners to begin with. Why did someone else think enough of them to make

62 Id., pp. 47, 60.

63 Helping you figure out your Unique Ability is beyond the scope of this book. For the process for figuring them out, see Id., Chapters 3-4.

a path for them to become co-owners of a family enterprise? Why did someone else have enough regard for them to benefit them in a trust?

Unique Ability is part of the answer. If the creator of the enterprise knew you when creating the enterprise, they likely saw flashes of your Unique Ability. They wanted to make a way to cultivate your Unique Ability. Even if they did not know exactly what your Unique Ability was—for example, you were a baby or a small child at the time—they wanted to offer you a way to develop your Unique Ability when the time came. And now the time has come.

Remember, Unique Ability applies to everyone in your family, not just you. Unique Ability exists in all the owners in your family. Not one of them lacks Unique Ability. Every person in your family, even the ones who irritate you the most, has Unique Ability. So, if every person is best off spending most of their time in their Unique Ability, then a family of co-owners is best off when all the co-owners spend most of their time in their respective Unique Ability. Instead of just one person using his or her Unique Ability, you have an entire extended family, each member using their respective Unique Ability. You have co-owners who are activated. You may even have a Unique Ability Team.

How does this work? To really dig into your Unique Ability, you must free yourself up. You must pare back all the activities at which you are less talented. For sure you should stop doing the things at which you are incompetent, and even the things at which you are merely mediocre. How do you free yourself to live out who you really are? Here are some examples.

YOU STOP[64]

Larry was the head of a family professional services company. When Covid-19 was raging in 2020, before monthly ownership meetings, he used to send his siblings electronic links to materials for the meetings. Larry was not good at preparing this detail. When he did it, he felt exhausted. His siblings did not seem to appreciate this additional work on his part. Once the pandemic ended, all his siblings but one resumed attending the meetings in person. The remote access links no longer were important. Rather than continue wearing himself out on a non-essential practice, Larry simply stopped doing it.

YOU DELEGATE

Paul, the CEO mentioned earlier in this chapter, does not attempt to handle everything that crosses his desk. He delegates surgically. For each task he delegates, he thinks of who in the family has the Unique Ability for the task. When planning meetings, he reserves to himself the tasks that fit his Unique Ability—for example, writing emails telling the group what he

64 Id., pp. 58-59.

wants to accomplish and what the agenda for the meeting will be. For other tasks associated with meetings that are not in his Unique Ability—such as scheduling the meeting, circulating the financial information, and preparing responses to co-owner questions—he looks to others whose Unique Ability fits the performance of these tasks. He sticks to his Unique Ability, and he relies on other people to use theirs.

YOU SWAP

Peter and Helen, brother and sister, take care of the family vacation place together. Helen is a worker. Her Unique Ability is hands-on labor. Peter is a planner. His Unique Ability is organizing the calendar for the extended family to use the place. Initially, Helen ran the calendar through a third party, which made the calendar inaccessible to Peter's side of the family. Meanwhile, Peter performed hands-on work he was not suited to perform. Peter and Helen swapped what they were doing. Peter turned over the hands-on work to Helen. Helen let Peter run the calendar. Now each of them does what they were meant to be doing.

YOU AUTOMATE

Herschel is trustee for a trust, set up by his father, that benefits himself and his two brothers. Over the past two years, Herschel's work calendar has gone out of control. His father is dead. Herschel's elderly mother complains he leaves too little time for family events. His children have given up trying to call him on the phone (and he has given up contacting them except by texting). Even worse, attention management is not part of Herschel's Unique Ability. He is distracted. He spends far too much time buried in his iPhone messages, even at dinner with his children. Recently, Herschel found a simple fix: he subscribed to an electronic appointment-setting system, where neither he nor his assistant sets meetings anymore. Herschel has reclaimed time for his family.

YOU CHANGE

Rebecca, mother of four, is her father's successor in the family land business. She is also superb at one-on-one time with each of her four children. She is a good cook, but she is not adept at cooking meals on the fly. Rather than trying to cook new meals every night when she comes home from work, she has started cooking ahead on weekends. At dinner time during the week, she thaws what she put in the freezer the previous Saturday. She likes the creativity of cooking, but even more she likes focused evening time with her children. As a result, the next day she feels more relaxed at the office.

These are examples of how Unique Ability helps a family owner get un-stuck. It's why Unique Ability has been called "the ultimate systems maximizer."[65]

UNIQUE ABILITY AND TRUSTS

Now it's time to apply Unique Ability to what we have learned about trusts. How does Unique Ability fit with family trusts?

As we explained in Chapter 5, the goal of every trust should be to put the people at the center. The trust should be run so it puts the system in service of the people. Unique Ability enhances this goal by allowing the people involved in the trust to develop themselves.

Here are examples for each person in a trust.

TRUST CREATOR

Recall Chapter 5's discussion of the importance of a trust's origins. Next to setting up a well-conceived trust, one of a trust creator's most important jobs is to be able to state *why* they set up the trust. What is the trust creator's connection to the beneficiaries? In what ways does the trust creator envision the trust could make the beneficiaries better off? How does the trust creator think the trust could protect the beneficiaries from being worse off?

65 Id., p. 207.

Many trust creators do not possess the Unique Ability to articulate, unprompted, the answers to these questions. A few do. But most, on their own, do not. (Neither do their advisors, which is doubly a problem.) They need prompting. How does a trust creator fix this problem? By finding someone who does have this Unique Ability, and enlisting that person to help the trust creator communicate what is on their mind. Such a person does not need to be a drafter of legal documents. Instead, the person needs to be superior at eliciting the trust creator's purpose and communicating it—in writing and orally, but especially in writing.

TRUSTEE

A trustee who has the Unique Ability of a teacher is a real find. Most good trustees are excellent at being organized. They keep accurate, thorough records. They know what the trust owns and what it's worth. They have receipts for deposits and stubs for distribution checks. But Unique Ability is more than being excellent. In addition to being organized, the best trustees have the mindset of a teacher.

To be an effective teacher of beneficiaries, first the trustee must be a student. The trustee must be willing to learn the trust agreement, appreciate what this particular trust can do for this particular group of beneficiaries, and most of all learn how serving as a fiduciary in this trust can help the trustee grow into an even better trustee.

After that, the trustee must actually *be* a teacher. The trustee must have the Unique Ability of putting in the time to help the beneficiary learn the trust. Optimally, the trustee has the Unique Ability of perceiving how the beneficiary learns and presenting information to the beneficiary according to how the beneficiary takes it in. If the trustee is not equipped to teach in a way that fits the beneficiary's learning style, the trustee should enlist someone whose Unique Ability is to zero in on the beneficiary's learning style. Either way, the trustee uses his or her Unique Ability to teach the beneficiary how to be a good beneficiary.

BENEFICIARY

To get a handle on a trust requires you to manage your attention—yes, manage your time, but even more, manage your attention. Recall Chapter 5: your attention is property you own.[66] In fact, it's probably the most valuable property you own. Focusing your attention develops your ownership of this irreplaceable piece of property that exists inside you.

As we saw in Chapter 5, the first way to use your attention is to read and learn the trust agreement. When you do not understand what the trust is saying, ask someone whose Unique Abili-

66 Dan Sullivan, *Your Attention: Your Property* (The Strategic Coach, Inc. 2021), p. 35.

ty is to explain the trust to you. Understand how the trust affects you. Start thinking about how you can integrate this trust into your life. How can you combine this trust with your Unique Ability to make something whole—both for yourself and those you affect every day? How can you harness your Unique Ability to meet the challenge of the Integrity Problem we raised in the Introduction to this book?

As you use your Unique Ability in this way, you will find you are thinking less like a consumer and more like an owner. When people criticize trusts as ruining beneficiaries, they are expressing revulsion at a consumerist culture. They see the trust as simply an ATM machine that enables the beneficiary to consume more and more. The beneficiary buys and spends, and buys and spends, in a pattern that renders that beneficiary's life wasteful, self-preoccupied, and under-developed.

UNIQUE ABILITY AND THE CONSUMING BENEFICIARY

No one should want trust beneficiaries who are just consumers. Not even beneficiaries should want this. Being merely a consumer eats people alive. The cycle of buying and spending, buying and spending is not rewarding. It enfeebles a beneficiary's body, and it offers no substance for the beneficiary's soul.

To be a Self-Governing Beneficiary, you must tackle head-on the problem of the beneficiary as a consumer.

To be fair, there are other ways to address this problem than by looking to Unique Ability. One way, which some beneficiary experts recommend, is simply to ignore the money in the trust. They suggest you live as though the money did not exist. They advocate forgetting the money is there.[67]

For example, Dora and Clarence, brother and sister, are trustees and beneficiaries of the same trust. The trust creator, their mother, is dead. Both Dora and Clarence have children. Dora and Clarence have two totally different views of money. Clarence sees money as a tool. He believes in inter-generational investing, and he likes using the trust to make investments that benefit generations younger than his. Dora, on the other hand, does not want to touch money more than absolutely necessary. She drives an old car, buys used clothes, and dislikes talking about investments. As the years passed, it became clear that Dora and Clarence did not agree on how to be a good trustee and how to be a good beneficiary. They simply didn't agree. Eventually Dora wrote Clarence a letter and told him two things. First, she said, she didn't want to be bound in the trust together. Second, she didn't want to make any plans based on the money in the trust. She wanted to live as if the trust and its assets did not exist. After some pointed conversations,[68] she and Clarence resolved their differences by splitting the trust. Clar-

67 See, for example, Thayer Cheatham Willis, *Beyond Gold: True Wealth For Inheritors* (New Concord Press 2012), pp. 240-241.

68 Scott, *Fierce Conversations*, pp. 5, 39.

ence's portion is geared to intergenerational investing and long-term growth. Dora's portion is designed to keep things quiet.

The question for beneficiaries like Dora is this: what happens at the end of your life, when you have decided not to come to terms with the trust, and now the money is set to pass to your descendants? The Integrity Problem is real. Deciding not to take steps to integrate the trust into your life has real consequences. Among these are:

- **Loss of financial value.** When people do not think about things they own, the condition of those things tends to deteriorate. If a trustee and a beneficiary do not think about a trust's investments, the value of those investments is likely to decrease because no one is paying attention to them. As the expression goes, "Out of sight, out of mind."

- **Accidental ingratitude.** Some trust beneficiaries are reluctant to draw on money in a trust because they want to respect the memory of the trust creator. Ironically, if the beneficiaries live as though the money is not present, they risk exhibiting a lack of gratitude. They ignore the gift the trust creator made to them.

- **Rupture of the past.** When you ignore a gift, you are refusing to appreciate how people who came before you developed their respective Unique Ability. They made you a gift because they earned and saved the money to create the gift. They earned and saved the money because they used their Unique Ability in ways that rewarded them monetarily. Their Unique Ability probably is an important example for you and your descendants to study. In addition, they are a part of your family history. If you don't know your origins, you will have trouble making sense of your present and your future.

- **Deception toward your descendants.** At some point, your descendants are going to find out about the money. They will wonder why you didn't think they were worth having a conversation with about this important subject. Plus, they will wonder why you lacked the courage to tell them the truth.[69]

- **Relinquishing opportunity.** As we saw in Chapter 3, whether you are a trustee or a beneficiary, you have the opportunity to designate the next steward of what you co-own.[70] If you live as though the money is not there, you throw away the opportunity to designate the next steward. In throwing away this opportunity, you are turning away from your role as Responsible Owner.

69 Scott, *Fierce Conversations.*

70 Blue, Splitting Heirs, p. 57.

The consumerist beneficiary lifestyle is a dead end. You can't avoid it by creating a supposed solution—avoiding the money altogether—that is itself a dead end. The only real solutions arise from what you have to work with. As a wise friend said to me many years ago, "We look to what is present, not to what is absent."

This is why a person's Unique Ability is so essential for integrating trusts and family co-ownership into your life. By using your Unique Ability to navigate the Integrity Problem, you will see the consumerist beneficiary lifestyle for the dead end it is. As you use your Unique Ability, you will develop a new, more valuable mindset. Your view of yourself, relative to the trust, will shift from, "How much do I get from the trust?" to "What effect will I have on the trust?"

The shift may not be quick, but it will be definite. And you will be better off.

FOCUS QUESTIONS

1. Have you ever taken a systematic look at your own Unique Ability? If so, go back to what you found last time you looked. If you haven't ever looked, get the Nomura book and follow the process in Chapters 3-4 of that book.

2. When it comes to your co-ownership with your family, what are the three things you most need to stop doing, to maximize the time you spend in your Unique Ability?

3. With regard to a trust you are involved in, what are the three things you most need to do to maximize your use of your Unique Ability?

4. What is the Unique Ability of each family co-owner who is most important to your future?

5. What are the most important things you need to do to designate and prepare the next steward of what you co-own?

CHAPTER SEVEN

ENTREPRENEURIAL STEWARDSHIP

"Families are unique in that they have no transactions or short-term events; they have only long-term transitions."

—JAMES E. HUGHES, JR.[71]

Stuart Lucas is the great-grandson of the founder of Carnation Milk. Stuart's great-grandfather, E.A. Stuart, started the company in 1899 after launching a prior business that failed. For 86 years the family owned the company, until in 1985 they sold it to Nestle for $3 billion.[72]

E.A. Stuart was a classic entrepreneur. He took risks, he was persistent, he surmounted obstacles. When his cans of evaporated milk spoiled, he figured out how to seal them better. When local customers did not see the need for his product, he sold it to gold prospectors in the Pacific Northwest. Just 10

71 Hughes, *Family: The Compact Among Generations*, p. 139.

72 Stuart Lucas, *Wealth: Grow It and Protect It* (FT Press 2013) (2nd ed.), pp. 1-3.

years after starting the company, he was selling 40 million cans of evaporated milk a year.[73]

Three generations later, his descendants needed different abilities to address very different problems. When the family sold Carnation, they were caught flat-footed. They had not planned on selling. They had not taken a coordinated approach to managing their money. They were accustomed to the business generating far higher returns on their money than the public markets could yield. In the 10 years after the sale, they started losing ground financially.[74]

Different challenges call for different solutions. Although Stuart Lucas is one of the leading experts on intergenerational family investing, he asserts that long-term, investing in the *human* capital of the family is more important than how the family invests its financial capital.[75]

Why? Because, as he says, "At its heart, family enterprise is about human capital, not just money."[76] Now obviously, there is no enterprise without a founding entrepreneur. If some hard-working person does not start an enterprise, there will be no enterprise down the road for succeeding generations. You must earn money before you have any money to save and spend. That's basic. But over multiple generations, Lucas asserts, "Family success ultimately resides in the actions of *descendants and*

73 Id. pp. 2-3.

74 Id., pp. 3-6.

75 Id., p. 22.

76 Id.

beneficiaries, not in the success of the founding entrepreneur."[77]

Think about that. Over the long term of a family, the family's descendants, and especially the beneficiaries of a trust, are more important for the overall success of the family than the person who got the ball rolling to begin with.

Think about that one more time. You, as a descendant of an entrepreneurial person, and you, as beneficiary of a family trust, are more important for how your family turns out long-term than the original entrepreneur was. You truly are at the center—far more than you realize.

This is why taking ownership of what you own is critical. This is why understanding your origins is critical. This is why being a good trust beneficiary is critical. This is why assessing the challenges facing *your* generation is critical.

ONE PERSON, TWO MISSIONS

This is where the concept of Entrepreneurial Stewardship comes in.[78] The concept combines two mindsets—an entrepreneur, and a steward—in the same person.

An entrepreneur is someone who takes resources from a

---

77 Id., p. 276 (emphasis added).

78 The concept of Entrepreneurial Stewardship is not original to me. The concept originated with Stuart Lucas, who taught it in a class in Private Wealth Management at the University of Chicago Booth School of Business, which I took in 2008.

lower level of productivity to a higher level of productivity.[79] An entrepreneur marshals resources in a way that makes them more valuable to other people. An entrepreneur accomplishes this by drawing on personal experiences, using his or her Unique Ability, having a sense of what other people count on him or her for, and sizing up advantages in both assets and situations. Above all, an entrepreneur works continuously from a position of creativity.

A steward, by contrast, is someone who looks after other people and their property. Four qualities characterize a steward:

1. A steward receives property gratefully. A steward is honored to have property placed with him or her. Taking charge of the property is an opportunity for the steward to use his or her Unique Ability, which the steward is happy to do. Receiving the property is a chance for the steward to be helpful.
2. A steward cares for the property responsibly. A steward takes care of the property as if it were their own. In this way, the steward also looks after the people who benefit from the property.
3. A steward draws forth the full value from the property. A steward does not let the property languish or become

79 Dan Sullivan, *Industry Transformers* (The Strategic Coach Inc. 2008), p. 7, quoting the definition created by French economist Jean-Baptiste Say in 1804.

unproductive. Recognizing the property's potential, the steward makes something happen with it—for the good of the other person and their family.

4. A steward returns the property more valuable than when the steward received it. The steward takes care of the property so effectively that when the steward is finished, the property is actually worth more than when the steward began.

An Entrepreneurial Steward is someone who has both the mindset of an entrepreneur and the mindset of a steward. He or she is both an improver of resources and a caretaker of persons and property. By working in both roles at the same time, an Entrepreneurial Steward lives two lives at once—the life of an enterprising person who pursues his or her own personal dream, and the life of a responsible person who inherits a dream of someone who came before him or her. The Entrepreneurial Steward lives two missions—one chosen, and one inherited.[80] It's not a simple way to go through life.

That's why not everyone in a family is cut out to be an Entrepreneurial Steward. An Entrepreneurial Steward is a family leader, someone who possesses drive and perspective, persistence and foresight, urgency and patience. Such a person is able to draw on the best of both the present and the past.

To appreciate how challenging this role is, think about risk.

80 Hughes, *Family: The Compact Among Generations*, pp. 189-194.

Risk for a start-up entrepreneur is very different than risk for a descendant of a successful entrepreneur. Someone who starts something from scratch has little to lose at the beginning. Typically the person has few financial resources and a lot of drive, ambition, and optimism. If the situation goes well, that person's descendants find themselves in a much different position. They have a lot to lose if they manage their assets poorly.[81] Plus, by this time there are more people in the family. More people equals more complexity. This is the point at which an Entrepreneurial Steward comes on the scene. An Entrepreneurial Steward needs to be able to handle both risk and complexity.

How does an Entrepreneurial Steward make this happen? Let's assume you are an Entrepreneurial Steward in your family. How specifically does your situation differ from the risk and complexity that someone who came before you faced?

Let's take a closer look.

ENTREPRENEURIAL STEWARDSHIP IN PRACTICE

Start-up entrepreneurs have ambition. They want to make something happen by creating value in a new way. They start at zero.

Descendants, by contrast, start with some financial advantages. They start at more than zero. This is a genuine advantage.

81 Id., pp. 276, 296.

Your challenge, as an Entrepreneurial Steward, is to treat this advantage as a resource, not a right.

Similarly, a start-up entrepreneur usually leads by telling other people what to do. At one of my son's second grade parent-teacher meetings, the teacher said, "Your son is never unsure of what to do." This is often true of start-up entrepreneurs. They have a vision in mind, and communicate the vision by telling others what needs to happen.

By contrast, a descendant, having more to lose, usually leads by seeking the opinions of others and melds them into a consensus.

Your challenge, as the descendant, is to know when to move between directive leading—telling people to do something—and consultative leading—helping the family arrive at a decision. You will need both.

INTEGRATED VISION FOR BOTH FAMILY AND BUSINESS

Start-up entrepreneurs are visionaries. They see possibilities and connections that others do not. Often they look upon the world from a mindset of wonder. However, this visionary outlook usually centers on business activity. A few entrepreneurs have an initial vision for family. But in most cases, they train their vision on business activity they want to conduct.

A descendant, by contrast, necessarily must deal with a vision for the family. Especially as the family grows in number, the descendants must consider who the people in the family need to be or become. The descendants must confront this question for at least their own household or their branch of the family.

Recall the Three-Circle Diagram from Chapters 3 and 5. In later generations of a family, ownership is usually de-centralized. Rather than one individual being the sole owner, a mix of individuals and trusts are the owners. These owners need a common vision for what they own. This is why Shared Purpose from Chapter 3 is indispensable.

For you, the Entrepreneurial Steward, the Integrity Problem involves a second layer. Not only must you integrate into your life the assets for which you are responsible. In addition, as Entrepreneurial Steward, you must lead your co-owners to integrate a vision for the assets with a vision for your family. This is a daunting task. It's not one the original entrepreneur had to face.

AIMING UP WHILE LOOKING BELOW

Start-up entrepreneurs go all-in on their business venture. Having little to lose, they take a big risk and maximize the upside potential of the venture.

A descendant, on other hand, faces the downside of possibly losing what the start-up entrepreneur built. A descendant cannot afford to concentrate risk in the way the original entrepreneur did. If things go wrong, all the success the original entrepreneur created could be wiped out.

As a result, you, as an Entrepreneurial Steward, must aim for upside potential at the same time you prepare your family to withstand downside loss. As Entrepreneurial Steward, you must diversify the risk. You must focus on new ways to make the family resources valuable, but not at the risk of losing the whole enterprise.

INTENTIONALLY DELAYED ENJOYMENT

Most start-up entrepreneurs do not begin with a lot of money. They do not enjoy financial success right away. E.A. Stuart, for example, tried and failed at one business before devising the idea of evaporated milk. Once he started Carnation, he had to contend with product failures and customers who didn't even see the point of his product.

A descendant of an entrepreneur usually occupies a far different position. The business venture succeeds, and the family acquires some money—sometimes a lot of money. The money is available for the family to buy what they want, when they want it.

You, an Entrepreneurial Steward, though, are different. You are in a position to enjoy spending money, but you delay the enjoyment on purpose. You see what is at stake. You recognize if you spend big now, you and your family—generations that come after you—will have less later.

CAREFUL WITH EXPENSES

Last, start-up entrepreneurs are frugal. You can't build a business if you're wasting the money to build it.

Descendants of an entrepreneur don't face this same financial pressure. They can afford not to care what things cost.

You, though, an Entrepreneurial Steward, are frugal on purpose. You can afford to spend. But you keep an eye on expenses so there is money left in the future.

THE ROLE OF UNIQUE ABILITY

What does Entrepreneurial Stewardship have to do with Unique Ability? A lot. Entrepreneurial Stewardship depends on Unique Ability. If no one in your family has the Unique Ability of either an entrepreneur or a steward, you will need to find people outside your family to help you stay afloat. On the other hand, if your family has multiple members who think like both an entrepreneur and a steward, you have the makings of a Unique Ability Team.

For example, in the Rice family, three members of the third generation think this way. A son, a daughter, and one son-in-law all have the mindsets of entrepreneur and steward. They work together to invest in real estate. The son is in charge of relationships with family members. The daughter oversees the financial accounting. The son-in-law manages the project staff. All of them love what they are doing. Even better, they find satisfaction in coupling their Unique Ability with the Unique Ability of each other.

TRUSTS AND ENTREPRENEURIAL STEWARDSHIP

You might think having access to a trust is a huge advantage for a family leader who aspires to be an Entrepreneurial Steward. The trust holds money, just sitting there waiting to be used on a new venture. There's no need to start a business to make the money. The money already is available.

Well, it's not that simple. There are at least three complications.

First, as we saw in Chapter 4, trustees are subject to laws, and rules in the trust agreement, about how to invest money. Trustees cannot invest in whatever they want, whenever they want. The trustee must keep an eye on both income for the current beneficiaries and principal for the remainder beneficiaries. Families tend to become larger over time. This means as the years pass, a family has more beneficiaries of the same trust. The money in the trust divides out among more people, not fewer. The longer the time a trust is set to run, and the more beneficiaries a trust has, the more this investment timeframe becomes an issue.

Second, a trustee is subject to laws requiring that trust assets be invested prudently, which usually means the assets must be diversified. Yet, as we saw in the example of E.A. Stuart, concentrating, and not diversifying, investment risk is how you build a successful entrepreneurial venture. Trusts are by nature conservative investors, not entrepreneurs.[82]

Third, if family members are permitted to become unaware of their roles as owners, even to the point that they don't know what they own, they become passive. They don't take charge. They don't use their Unique Ability. They remain ignorant of the potential of Entrepreneurial Stewardship. They assume the trust will run on autopilot, and they defer to the trustee. As a result, the trust causes the family's human capital—maybe not its financial capital, but its human capital—to decrease, not increase.[83]

This is why helping people in your family appreciate their roles as owners is critical. You can't blame all your problems on the fact that a trust exists. A trust is about possibilities. A trust is about human relationships. A trust is there because you were given an opportunity to be a beneficial owner. That's what the concept of split ownership is all about.

It's time to look at a tool called The Family Bank.

---

82 Hughes, *Family: The Compact Among Generations*, pp. 174-176.

83 Hughes, Complete Family Wealth, pp. 30, 32.

CHAPTER SEVEN

THE FAMILY BANK

A family bank is money provided from family members, set aside for the specific purpose of loaning money to other family members. Rather than borrowing money from a public bank, the family members borrow money from each other. A family bank is not regulated by the federal government. A family bank's loans must comply with IRS rules for intra-family loans. But there are no accounts, no depositors, and no funds available to the public, as at a regular bank. Instead, a family bank runs based on rules the family sets for itself.[84]

For example, using a family bank, a family could loan money from an older generation to younger generations to finance equipment for a summer job, rent an apartment during college, obtain a mortgage for a first home, or procure debt or equity financing to start a business.[85]

A family bank is not a pool of money to be doled out willy-nilly. It follows rules the family creates and enforces, especially rules for repaying loans.

Nor is a family bank a pool of money for making gifts. Family members may make gifts to each other at any time. But that's not how a family bank runs. Money in a family bank is not free.[86]

---

84 Warner King Babcock, "How to Properly Structure and Govern a Family Bank," *Trusts & Estates*, April 12, 2013.

85 Warner King Babcock, "Family Banks: Using Corporate Entities and Trusts," *Trusts & Estates*, July 3, 2013.

86 Babcock, "Family Banks: Using Corporate Entities and Trusts."

With a family bank, the borrower writes up a loan application, just as if borrowing money from a regular bank. If wanting to start a business, the borrower also includes a written business plan. The borrower reviews the proposed loan with the family bank's board of operators. The bank lends the money to the family member, who updates the board on the investment the bank has made. The borrower pays back the loan.

A family bank is a family enterprise, in the sense that it's a project family members work on together. There are many ways to structure this enterprise. Some people may use money segregated within a part of one trust. Other families may use money from multiple trusts. One recommended way is to have a trust own a limited liability company that makes the loans using money from the trust. Members of your family run the company. To make sure the company has the advantage of independence, you might want to have a couple of non-family members help run it.[87]

When considering which structure to use, don't let structure obscure the larger purpose. There are two reasons to set up a family bank. The first is investment of the family's financial capital—to increase the value of the family's financial assets. The second is development of the family's non-financial capital—to increase the depth and usefulness of the human, intellectual, social and spiritual capital of the people in the family.[88] The goal

87 Id.

88 Hughes, *Complete Wealth*, pp. 156-158; see Chapter 1, about the relationship of family capital to interconnections outside the family.

is to help everyone in the family become more aware of their status as owners, more interested in the potential of ownership, and more independent.

In this way, a family bank enables the family to invest in the Unique Ability of people within its ranks. For example, in one family is a grandson talented in computer animation. The family loans money to him for him to start his own film animation company. The board of the family bank helps him refine his business plan and puts him in touch with experts who help hone his strategy. As business becomes profitable, the grandson repays the loan from cash flow from the business. The grandson now thinks like an owner.

Even more, when the time comes for the grandson to receive distributions from a trust outside the family bank, the grandson is prepared. He appreciates how to receive financial assistance, and he is driven to make something happen. He is ready to apply the principles of Entrepreneurial Stewardship.

THE ROLE OF COURAGE

Discovering and using your Unique Ability requires courage. So does appreciating and applying the principles of Entrepreneurial Stewardship. Being a good trust beneficiary, with the goal of being an Entrepreneurial Steward, is a courageous act.

Recall the Introduction to this book. Courage is required

because the interplay of family and money tends to make people fearful. You fear not living up to the hopes and expectations of those who came before you. You fear being unworthy of the gift of money they placed in trust for you. You fear them criticizing you for what you do with the money. You fear finding out your Unique Ability. Yet you fear living your whole life without putting your Unique Ability to use. And so on.

When faced with fear, you have but two choices: courage, and courage avoidance.[89] Courage avoidance takes many forms: denying the facts, refusing to listen, withdrawing into one's self, disregarding another person's well-being, seeking to impress others for the wrong reasons, misplacing a desire for human relationship.

Courage, on the other hand, always proceeds from one thing: telling the truth. The courageous person admits what he or she is actually thinking and feeling.[90]

Courage, however, first requires an act of commitment. You are not courageous until you commit to taking specific action that will affect your future.[91]

Using your Unique Ability, especially when you occupy the role of Entrepreneurial Steward, is the best way to apply courage and overcome fear. Fear is natural. Fortunately, so is your

89 Dan Sullivan, *The Four C's Formula* (The Strategic Coach Inc. 2015), p. 8. For examples of courage where you are responsible for the lives of others, see Omar N. Bradley, *A General's Life* (Simon and Schuster 1983).

90 Sullivan, *The Four C's Formula*, p. 8.

91 Id., Chs. 1-2; Scott, *Fierce Conversations*.

Unique Ability. When raising the courage to take action, you use your Unique Ability—not someone else's, but yours. You display courage by implementing your Unique Ability.

For example, when E.A. Stuart's first business failed, he needed to be courageous to start an evaporated milk company. When local farmers did not see the point of buying evaporated milk, Stuart needed courage to go to where the market was: gold prospectors who were moving into the Pacific Northwest. Stuart used his Unique Ability to surmount these challenges. Decades later, Stuart's grandchildren and great-grandchildren needed to be courageous in confronting their stagnating investment returns and firing their bank. They drew on a different Unique Ability to change course.[92]

A person's Unique Ability never goes out of style. Neither does the practice of Entrepreneurial Stewardship. You and your family always need both, no matter how many people or generations your family encompasses.

COURAGE AND THE NEXT STEWARD

In Chapter 3, we looked at how being a Responsible Owner™ reflects your human agency as owner of important assets. You exercise authority over what you own. One unique important exercise of this authority is naming the next steward.

92 Lucas, *Wealth: Grow It and Protect It.*

You are not going to live forever. You may live a long time. But at some point, you, I, and everyone reading this book will be deceased. If you are serious about choosing for what you own, you need to think about, and provide for, who will be the next steward after you.

This question involves two layers:

1. **After you, who will be the next stewards of what you own?**

Optimally, everyone in your family will develop the mindset of a steward. But some may not. Of those who do have the mindset of a steward, you need to decide which ones should be responsible for what. Not everyone is authoritative with respect to everything. You need to decide which people in your family should be responsible for what.

2. **Among the people in your family, who are best situated to be the next Entrepreneurial Stewards?**

An Entrepreneurial Steward is a family leader who has drive, persistence, foresight, and both patience and a sense of urgency. Not every person in a family is cut out for this role. Not every steward is an Entrepreneurial Steward. You need to consider the Unique Ability of every person in your family. Who is able to serve as an Entrepreneurial Steward? How will this person interact with others in the family who have the mindset of a steward?

Choosing the next steward, and cultivating the next Entrepreneurial Steward, is not simple or easy. That's one reason you need courage.

AMBITION RIGHTLY UNDERSTOOD

Before concluding this chapter, we need to tackle one other topic: ambition. Many people today are highly critical of families who have financial capital. Such families are seen as greedy, selfish, unprincipled, needy, pathetic, and most of all, "dysfunctional." One reason for this caricature is that when families do deal successfully with the Integrity Problem, their success does not make the news. The public does not hear about it.[93] Regardless of what the public hears, ambition is not necessarily a bad word. Honorable ambition is entirely consistent with being a family owner.[94]

Being honorably ambitious, using your Unique Ability, and practicing Entrepreneurial Stewardship, requires you to take a stand. You take steps in favor of using what you have. You signal that you are drawing on resources available to you.

Taking a stand may bring public attention. My friend, Rex, is the son-in-law of a second generation owner of a company his

93 For a counterpoint to the popular view of families and money, see Grubman, *Wealth 3.0.*

94 Robert Faulkner, *The Case For Greatness: Honorable Ambition and Its Critics* (Yale University Press 2007).

in-laws sold years ago. When the family used money from the sale to buy real estate in a depressed part of town, Rex quit his job to run the new real estate business. Improving the properties involved dealing with urban crime. As crime waves hit the neighborhood, Rex spent Saturday mornings personally cleaning graffiti from buildings and assuring safety for residents. Rex was quoted in the news. Now, many people know Rex's family is a prominent landlord. Some may resent Rex. But Rex has taken a stand, in favor of revitalizing a neighborhood, providing housing, encouraging restaurants and retail stores, and showing what is possible.

To take another example: Kathleen runs a private foundation, started by her aunt, focused on elementary and high school education reform. The foundation adopted a small, broken-down elementary school that had declining enrollment in a poor neighborhood. To fix the enrollment problem, Kathleen personally went door to door and asked mothers in the neighborhood to consider challenging their children with the new curriculum at the school. The mothers said yes. Enrollment rose from 60 to 250. The foundation was asked to take on a second school. Kathleen is now known as someone who can fix school problems. Some people like her for this. Some don't. She takes action anyway.

When people like Rex and Kathleen take a stand, they go against the criticism that America is full of people who act out of self-interest alone. The criticism is that Americans are not genuinely virtuous, that they merely exploit opportunities for greed and control.[95] One problem with this criticism (there are many) is its failure to distinguish between greed and acquisitiveness.[96] A greedy person is preoccupied with possessing things. To the greedy person, the more things you possess, the better. The way you get control of them is not important. The goal is simply to seize them for yourself so other people cannot take them from you.

An acquisitive person, by contrast, is more interested in the process of earning things, especially earning them justly.[97] The process of acquiring is not divorced from justice. An acquisitive person is more interested in earning than possessing, because earning is how you perform work that is valuable for other people. Yes, an acquisitive person is interested in owning things, but owning them as a result of hard work, willingness to take risks, diligence, and waiting to receive the benefits of their labor. Frugality and prudence also come into play here. Together, these qualities form habits that establish a life of some genuine virtues—in each person, in their communities, and in their country.[98]

Optimally, all these good qualities come together in a Re-

95 Martin Diamond, "Ethics and Politics – The American Way," in *As Far As Republican Principles Will Admit: Essays by Martin Diamond* (AEI Press 1992), pp. 356-358.

96 Id., pp. 359-360.

97 Id., p. 360.

98 Id., pp. 360-363; Faulkner, *The Case for Greatness – Honorable Ambition and Its Critics*, Ch. 2.

sponsible Owner.™

Here's an example of how honorable ambition manifests itself in a Responsible Owner. About seven years ago, I was taking an Uber to a business meeting in Phoenix, Arizona. Though late spring, the day was very hot—well into the upper 90s. Driving the car was a young man, a Russian whose family had lived in Russia for generations. Once the Soviet Union collapsed, his family began a journey of immigration that ended with settling in Pennsylvania. Being adventurous in his 20s, he decided to move to Arizona, where he and his brother started a self-storage facility business. Not wanting to waste his spare time, he picked up extra cash driving for Uber. From these business activities, he used some of his earnings to support relatives back in Pennsylvania and abroad.

I asked him why he had chosen to live this unusual life in the middle of the desert, on a furnace-hot day such as this. Why, I asked him, did he undertake all of this?

He paused, then said quietly, "Because I wanted to try my hand at the American dream."

Think back to Chapter 3, where we talked about communicating your dreams in terms of your ambition. This man had a dream, and he was ambitious to pursue it. Though an earlier-stage business owner than E.A. Stuart, and working on a much smaller scale than Stuart, he had achieved some financial success. He co-owned the self-storage facilities with his brother. He did not make all the decisions, but he was authoritative as to part of the business. Certainly he was authoritative as to his own life in the United States. He was a Responsible Owner.

In conclusion, here's a quick test:

Does developing your Unique Ability, and positioning your family to practice Entrepreneurial Stewardship, require ambition? Absolutely yes.

Does taking these steps necessarily mean you and your family are greedy, self-interested people who aren't doing anything genuinely good? Absolutely not.

And does it mean that your life, and the long-term success of your family, is about anything more than money? Again, absolutely yes. Confronting the Integrity Problem requires ambition—plenty of humility, but ambition too. Drawing on your ambition is part of developing the non-financial capital of you and your family—the very capital your family needs most in the long run.

So forge ahead, confident you have abilities unique to you alone, which position you to develop the mindsets of both entrepreneur and steward, and build up the value beyond money that is the stuff of real ownership.

FOCUS QUESTIONS

1. Think of human capital as the people who comprise your family. What needs to be done to develop this human capital?

2. Does your family have an Entrepreneurial Steward? If you do, what can be done to cultivate this person's Unique Ability? If you don't, what can be done to identify and develop such a person?

3. What is the most courageous act you can perform for your family in the next 12 months?

4. How would you describe your ambition as a family owner?

5. What are the three most important things you need to do in the next 12 months to position your family to practice Entrepreneurial Stewardship?

CHAPTER EIGHT

THE PRINCIPLES IN ACTION

"It is not the critic who counts. The credit belongs to the man who is actually in the arena."

—THEODORE ROOSEVELT, APRIL 23, 1910[99]

So far in this book, we've looked at a set of concepts that help you confront and resolve the Integrity Problem. After showing the implications of ownership and setting out the contours of a family enterprise, we looked at Shared Purpose and the idea of being a Responsible Owner. Then we learned how trusts work, and we considered trusts in parallel to a journey where you develop the mindset of a Self-Governing Beneficiary. After that, we looked at the concept of Unique Ability among family co-owners. Then we reviewed the concept of Entrepreneurial Stewardship and its importance for later co-owners in a family.

99 Theodore Roosevelt, "Citizenship In A Republic," speech at The Sorbonne, Paris, France, April 23, 1910. See https://www.presidency.ucsb.edu/documents/address-the-sorbonne-paris-france-citizenship-republic.

Principles are essential, but they're not much good if you don't use them. In this chapter, we look at these principles in action, with an eye toward using them.

As we look, bear in mind that the family in this chapter is meant to be realistic. This means that just like your family, none of the people in this family is perfect. In the field of trusts and family enterprise ownership, being an armchair quarterback, where you critique the plays without ever running any yourself, is too easy. Everyone has an answer for what should be done. Actually doing it is quite different than talking about it.

Fortunately, knowing the principles gives you a framework for deciding how to act in your own family. With this chapter, the hope is that you, the reader, having studied the principles, now will come up with your own answers for how things could be done, both in this example family and your own family. After you finish the chapter, be sure to look at the Focus Questions for it.

MEET THE OUSTALETS

Richard Oustalet is 82 years old. He lives in a suburb of a major Midwestern city with his second wife, Camille.

Richard's first wife, Emily, was the only child of John R. Land. Mr. Land was a real estate developer who, over the course of six decades, created a very profitable portfolio of suburban office buildings and apartments. Mr. Land was a low-profile investor. He kept his name out of the news. He did not create a big holding company. Instead, he owned each property as a separate entity, with all the entities having the common connection of him as sole owner.

When Mr. Land's daughter, Emily, married Richard, Richard went to work for his father-in-law. Mr. Land was a hands-on operator, and Richard learned from him.

Once Richard and Emily married, Richard never worked anywhere but in Mr. Land's business. Richard worked there continuously until Mr. Land died, three decades later. During this entire time, Richard never was an owner of the business. Neither was Emily. But Mr. Land paid Richard well, and Richard and Emily were content.

During the whole time Richard worked in his father-in-law's business, Emily did other things. She preferred not to be involved in the business.

Mr. Land himself worked full-time until he was 83 years old, when he had a stroke. When the stroke happened, Richard took over all aspects of the business. Mr. Land continued to be the sole owner, and Richard asked his opinion on important issues, but Richard ran things.

Mr. Land's stroke uncovered a problem. Mr. Land was talented at buying real estate, but he wasn't the best at planning for its ownership. He disliked talking about himself, and he especially disliked thinking about death—his or anyone else's. When he died at age 87, he simply left all the properties outright to Emily. The deeds for the properties went from Mr. Land individually to Emily individually. Although Mr. Land saw this solution as simple, his property portfolio was valuable enough that his estate ended up owing federal estate tax. The tax payment upset Emily tremendously. Now that she owned the properties, she vowed she would structure her own estate differently.

TWO MORE GENERATIONS

Richard and Emily had married in their late 20s. In their 30s, they had three sons—Richard Jr., Jerry, and Leonard. Despite growing up in a relatively affluent household, all three sons worked productively starting in their late teen years.

Richard Jr. went to work with his father and grandfather in the real estate business.

Jerry found real estate boring. He moved to California and went into sales for a chain of retail tire stores.

Leonard stayed in town and became a dentist.

All three sons married and had children. Richard Jr. and his wife, Angie, had five children. They had four sons of their own—Richard III, Henry, Mack, and John. They also adopted a little girl, Sarah. Jerry and his wife, the noted Hollywood movie distributor Erica Enright, had three children, all girls—Helene, Desdemona, and Korson. Leonard and his wife, Lenora, had one child, a daughter named Tootie.

John R. Land lived to see the great-grandchildren. Though he had always focused mostly on his work, he enjoyed getting to know these new people in the family. Years earlier, Mr. Land had purchased a house on a lake in northern Wisconsin. Several times a year, he would sneak up there for vacations. Now he was pleased for his children, grandchildren and great-grandchildren to join him.

In just four generations, the family had increased from three people (John R. Land, his wife, and Emily) to 19, spread across five households and two states.

ANOTHER DEATH

When Emily inherited the properties after her father died, she kept her father's management structure in place. She asked Richard to manage the business, just as he had before. The properties continued to cash flow well, and Emily and Richard prospered. Emily realized she needed to plan better than her father for transferring the ownership. Whereas Mr. Land had left the properties to Emily outright, Emily placed each property in a separate limited liability company (LLC) and created a set of trusts to own all the companies.

For the main trust, she named herself and Richard as co-trustees. For beneficiaries, she named herself, then Richard, and then Richard Jr., Jerry, and Leonard in equal shares. Under this trust, the three sons would not benefit until both she and

Richard were deceased.

However, Emily also created three other trusts, one to benefit each son and his respective descendants. She and Richard Jr. were co-trustees of the trust to benefit Richard Jr. and his descendants. She and Jerry were co-trustees of the trust to benefit Jerry and his descendants. She and Leonard were co-trustees of the trust to benefit Leonard and his descendants. If Emily no longer could serve as trustee, the sons were to become sole trustees of their respective trusts. Under these three trusts, each son benefited at the same time Emily and Richard did.

Emily then split the LLC ownership into voting and nonvoting units, with the four trusts holding the nonvoting units and a separate LLC owning the voting units. Emily's trust owned most of the nonvoting units. The three trusts for the sons owned minority stakes. Emily kept ownership of this voting unit LLC for herself.

The result was that Emily retained voting control over the LLCs, and the trusts were entitled to distributable cash from the rental income the LLCs generated. Emily, as manager of the master LLC, decided when to distribute cash from the business. As cash was distributed, income flowed to her and Richard by way of Emily's trust, and to each son by way of the trusts Emily set up for them.

Emily created this new ownership arrangement for three reasons. First, she wanted to avoid her father's problem of paying federal estate tax at her death. Second, she wanted beneficial ownership of the portfolio to be roughly equal among her three sons when she and Richard died. Third, she wanted each son to have some experience of beneficial ownership during her lifetime, not just after she and Richard were gone.

Last, because Emily wanted to benefit certain charities in the community, and she was adamant that money go to charity rather than taxes, she set up a donor advised fund. She named herself the fund advisor, with Richard as successor fund advisor.

Unfortunately, Emily counted on living longer than she did. She died of heart failure at age 63, just three years after her father died.

Emily's death flattened Richard. He didn't know what to do with himself. Financially he was fine. He was still an employee of the business, and as beneficiary of Emily's trust, he received a majority of the income from the business's profits. But in all other ways he felt empty. Richard Jr. and Angie, living nearby, stayed in close touch and brought their children over to visit frequently. Leonard's wife, Lenora, cooked family dinners for the group. The three sons—Richard Jr., Jerry, and Leonard—also made a point to take Richard on fishing trips to the house in northern Wisconsin.

Eventually Richard met a congenial woman, Camille Alvarez, whom he married. Camille's first husband had left her years ago, and alone she had raised a daughter, Claudine. Claudine, now in her early 30s, had started her work life cleaning floors at a Wendy's restaurant in Tennessee. Eventually she became a store manager and an accountant. Then she earned a law degree at a night law school. She parlayed this combined experience into a job overseeing operations for a franchisee of restaurant brands.

THINKING ABOUT THE FUTURE

Happily married to Camille, and nearing age 70, Richard Oustalet started thinking seriously about ownership. He was the primary person responsible for three significant assets that affected his family: the real estate business, the vacation property in Wisconsin, and the donor advised fund.

Richard had some idea what he wanted. The properties still cranked out reliable distributions. The Wisconsin property was worth far more than when his father in law had bought it. The donor advised fund made grants to charities important to him. Richard knew he wanted to keep all three going.

Yet Richard had a problem: he didn't know what his children wanted. He didn't know how to talk to his family, and especially his three sons, about what they wanted. As trustees and beneficiaries of the other trusts, they co-owned the business with Richard. Precisely because Richard was trustee of Emily's trust and he controlled the voting units in the master LLC, Richard felt uneasy about talking to his sons. He didn't want them to feel as though he was lording control over them. Plus, they had taken such good care of him when Emily died, and he didn't feel right about suggesting a plan they, his co-owners, would not endorse.

So, Richard said nothing. He wanted to say something, but he didn't know how.

CHANGES IN THE MARKET

Life changed for the Oustalets in February 2020, when Covid-19 hit the United States. Every member of the family had to change what they were doing, and change drastically.

In the real estate business, Richard and Richard Jr. could barely keep up with the new environment for tenants. The government told people to distance themselves and take every precaution, so employees of nearly all the tenant businesses in Oustalet buildings stayed home. The tenants called Richard asking for rent reductions, abatements, and other drastic changes. Richard, now in his 70s, was working 70 hour weeks trying to calm the tenants. Richard Jr. was working 85 hour weeks dealing with the bank, lawyers, and the insurance underwriter.

For the first time since John R. Land acquired the first piece of real estate, the business did not distribute any cash to its owners. None of the trusts received any distributions.

Panicked, Richard Jr. told Richard they needed help from someone who really understood the owners.

Their solution? Call Claudine. She had an accounting background, she was good at operations, and she was scrappy.

After consulting Camille, Richard offered Claudine a job working with Richard Jr. in the business. For Claudine, this meant a pay increase, a big challenge, and an appealing chance to grow closer to the family into which her mother had married. Claudine said yes.

Even with Claudine on the management team, the office side of the portfolio continued to deteriorate. Because the Oustalets' buildings were in mostly suburban locations, their tenants returned to the spaces more quickly than tenants of large downtown buildings. But the economic effects of the pandemic lingered a long time. Three years later, the commercial real estate market was suffering from high interest rates. Few people were lining up to buy office buildings, and all buyers were demanding discounts, some steep.

Fortunately, the multi-family side of the business remained strong. The high interest rates drove apartment renters to stay put rather than move out and buy houses with big mortgages.

On balance, though, the portfolio assembled over decades by John R. Land simply wasn't worth as much as it had been. As manager of the master LLC, Richard decided to distribute some cash to the trusts, but significantly less than in past years.

TIME TO START TALKING

Having worked closely with Richard Jr. and Claudine during the pandemic, and seeing all the more what was at stake,

Richard decided to make the first move on family communications. He convened a meeting of his three sons, their wives, and the grandchildren. At the meeting, he identified the three big assets—the real estate portfolio, the Wisconsin house, and the donor advised fund. He explained that now, in his early 80s, he wanted to make sure the assets were positioned to support the family over the long term. He proposed the following:

- At his death, Emily's trust was set to divide into equal shares for Richard Jr., Jerry and Leonard. The trust already allowed each son to redirect his share, so as to benefit the son's descendants using either the existing trusts for the sons or new trusts the sons would create for themselves. Richard recommended his sons plan for this.

- The voting units for the master LLC would be controlled by a committee of three—Richard Jr., Claudine, and a third family member elected by the trustees of the sons' trusts.

- The Wisconsin property would go into a family LLC owned by the three branches. The LLC would allow step-children to participate on the same basis as blood descendants.

- At Richard's death, the successor fund advisor for the donor advised fund would consist of three family members, one elected from each branch.

Richard added that he hadn't confronted all the questions. Under Emily's trust, he had the right to appoint his own successor trustee. He wasn't sure whom to appoint. He also wasn't satisfied the business had developed a realistic policy for distributing cash to the trusts as owners. He also wanted his sons to be ready for Emily's trust to split into shares at his death. Most of all, Richard worried about how the business would remain profitable enough to provide income to the growing number of descendants across multiple generations. But he thought an 80% plan was better than none, and he wanted to start a conversation with the family.

Richard sat back and waited for reactions.

No one disagreed outright with him. All the children appreciated what he intended, though some were less interested than others. Five years ago, Jerry had become the Chief Operating Officer and a significant shareholder of the California tire store chain, which actually had grown significantly during the pandemic. Jerry was consumed with his work, even while he was trustee of the trust Emily set up for him and his branch. By contrast, Leonard's dental practice had been decimated by Covid. Even though the practice had recovered, Leonard appreciated the focus on the future, especially opportunities for the grandchildren to work in the business.

However, the sons were confused about the trusts. They didn't understand how money came out of the business through the trusts. Nor did they know how Emily's trust was going to operate at Richard's death. They agreed to get together and study the four trusts, and then work with Richard to develop a plan for distributions.

Everyone liked the plan for Wisconsin, even though Erica Enright secretly wondered whether she and Jerry would want to be bought out.

As for the donor advised fund, they all thought the successor fund advisor plan was fair.

Among the grandchildren, Richard III, Mack, and Helene voiced interest in quitting their jobs and working in the business. Richard was elated to hear this, though he cautioned they would need to create some kind of family employment policy. This, he explained, was a good problem to have.

Afterward, Richard Jr. asked his father about the fact that neither Camille nor Claudine were beneficiaries of any of the trusts. Emily had set up the trusts not expecting to die prematurely, and obviously she had not intended to benefit a new wife or step-daughter for Richard. Richard responded that as Camille's husband, he shared his trust distributions with her. As for Claudine, who was now a key figure in the business, Richard suggested they set up a non-stock compensation plan for her, under which she would share in the value of the portfolio. Richard Jr. thought this was an excellent idea.

POINTS TO PONDER

Let's stop for a moment. How does the Oustalets' situation illustrate the concepts presented in this book? Here are some points to consider:

- Complexity is real. The Oustalets are not a large family, yet they have a lot going on. There is complexity in number of people. There are four generations—from John R. Land, the great-grandfather, to nine great-grandchildren—Richard III, Henry, Mack, John, Sarah, Helene, Desdemona, Korson, and Tootie—across three branches. There is also complexity of location. One branch of the family lives out of town, doesn't see the others often, and is financially independent of the family business. Last, there is complexity in enterprise. The Oustalets have three enterprises—a real estate business, a vacation property, and a donor advised fund. Combined, these generate a lot of activity. As the family moves to a fourth generation, these complexities are likely to increase, not decrease.

- Scarcity is real. No matter how much money is involved

in a family, there is never enough money to do everything one might want without limit. John R. Land acquired solid pieces of real estate, yet the pandemic crippled the business in ways he and Richard never envisioned. The business has not yet returned to generating the returns it used to.

- Death is unexpected for some and certain for all. John R. Land died in his 80s after a long, full life. Yet his daughter, Emily, died just three years after him, at age 63.

- In-laws can be an advantage. Often a blood child does not like another child's spouse. Equally often, it seems, the relationship between mother-in-law and daughter-in-law is strained. Yet in-laws can bring a new variety of Unique Ability to a family. In the second generation, Richard Oustalet was the worker behind his father-in-law's vision. In the third generation, Claudine Oustalet came up the hard way. Yet Claudine had Unique Ability others in the family did not, abilities the family needed when the real estate market tilted, and the family respected her. If the great-grandchildren join the business, they may end up reporting to her.

- Including non-owners can be tricky. None of the Oustalets desired to exclude Richard's second wife, Camille, and her daughter, Claudine. Yet because Emily Oustalet was the one who set up the trusts, the family had to figure out new ways economically to include Camille and Claudine.

- The dream of one family member may not be the dream of another. John R. Land loved real estate. Richard Oustalet loved working in the business. Grandsons Jerry and Leonard, by contrast, wanted to do their own thing. In Jerry's case, the tire store venture rewarded him financially more than the family back home expected.

- Happy endings are not guaranteed, but time is an advantage for those who are patient with it and themselves.[100] Recognizing that the changing real estate market demanded new long-term thinking, Richard Oustalet marshalled the family to use the time available to them.

- The existence of the Integrity Problem does not mean something is wrong with you. It does not necessarily

100 Karol Wojtyla, *The Jeweler's Shop*, Three-act play, translated by Boleslaw Taborski (Ignatius Press 1992).

mean you are troubled or weak. It just means you are honest. When you own something valuable enough to pass on, you must figure out how to integrate what you own and who you are.

THE FUTURE AND CONFIDENCE

The following Thanksgiving, the Oustalet family had dinner at Richard Jr. and Angie's house. In the past, Richard and Camille had hosted. This year, they offered the host role to Richard Jr. and Angie, who were genuinely happy to take it on. Jerry and his family flew in from California. Leonard and Lenora brought smoked turkey that Leonard himself fixed.

Someone jokingly posed the question, "How many Thanksgivings does any of us have left?"

The Oustalets' consensus was that although none of them knew the future, they felt grateful for how they had navigated the past and confident in what they needed to do next.

FOCUS QUESTIONS

1. **Have you mapped out how many more people will likely be in your family in the next two generations (by the time you are a grandparent)? If not, use the blank Three-Circle Model on page [TK] of this book, and place on the Model all the people who are likely to be in your family by that time.**

2. **What has been the most consequential death in your family? How did you deal with it?**

3. **How does your family treat in-laws? How, if at all, should the status of in-laws change in your family?**

4. **What is the biggest downside risk facing your family?**

5. **If you want to undertake the dream of someone else in your family, what are three specific steps you need to perform to undertake it?**

CONCLUSION

YOU, THE INTEGRATED OWNER

"A people without history is not redeemed from time, for history is a pattern of timeless moments."

—T.S. ELIOT, "LITTLE GIDDING," FOUR QUARTETS

I live in a 100 year old farmhouse. It was built in 1904; the land, though, goes back many more years than that. The first deed for the property dates to January 8, 1833. That's only 30 years after Ohio became a state, and nearly 30 years before Americans fought one another in the Civil War.

The original parcel of property for my house was 160 acres. For 75 years, from 1859 to 1934, one family farmed this acreage. In fact, multiple generations of this one family owned it. They're the ones who built the house.

All of this came to light when my wife and I were remodeling our kitchen a few years ago. The kitchen space spanned two areas, the original house and a rear addition, and had been constructed in two different ways. To remodel the whole space correctly, the contractor needed to pare it back to the original wall facings.

That's when we found it.

In the old part of the kitchen, the contractor unearthed old, old wallpaper. Judging from the colors, the images and the style, the paper was from the 1910s or 1920s. Was this wallpaper original to the house? Maybe. We stared at it for several days, mostly from curiosity, and then let the contractor place drywall over it. No one removed the wallpaper. It's still there.

The wallpaper surprise was a reminder that no owner of anything—not a house, not land, not cash, not anything else valuable—is the only owner that thing will ever have. There was an owner before you. There will be an owner after you. At least seven families owned my house before my wife and I came along. Someday, after we stop owning the house, someone new will take over.

No matter which owner you are in the chain, there is never a time you may put your ownership on autopilot. Ownership is not like washing clothes in a full-automatic, microchip-powered washer. Ownership is not a "set it and forget it" activity.

On the contrary, ownership calls for foresight, to spot both the future upsides and the future downsides. My house, for example, went through difficulties. In the 1970s, the house went through a bankruptcy. In the 1990s, the house went through an embarrassing divorce. You can bet the owner in the 1970s did not want to go through personal bankruptcy, nor did the owner in the 1990s want her husband to leave her for a much younger woman. Yet these things happen—and they are not the end. The 1970s owner emerged from bankruptcy and lived in the house for another five years. The 1990s owner kept the house in the divorce, remarried a wonderful man, and lived there for another 16 years. Human beings are more resilient than they expect.

I like to think the house itself has provided resilience for its owners. Its construction is unique. Starting just above the foundation, and going all the way to the peak of the attic roof, the outside walls are built of field stone mortared together in square blocks. The original builder created a square form, placed the field stone inside, mixed in some mortar, flipped the form on its side, and set it in place—one square above the other, all the way up to the attic. I've never seen another house built this way.

The stone means this house is not going anywhere. About six years ago, we experienced a near-tornado. The weather service directed everyone to the basement, and we went. The tornado sirens activated. We could hear a loud roaring noise coming up the valley from the west. After the storm subsided, we went outside to find...no damage. Fallen trees blocked the road in both directions. The roofs of houses down the road were torn off. Trees in front of those houses were swirled into toothpicks and split down the middle. The whole place was a mess for several days. But our house stood. It protected us.

Protection is one thing; flexibility is another. Our house has been added onto at least three times—once for a porch and wood siding across the front (apparently the owners in the 1940s didn't care for a front-on stone look), and twice for additions to the back. Subsequent owners needed more space, and the original house was flexible enough to accommodate the need. These additions enhanced the structure, with more room, more natural light, and more features. The house has adapted to fit the needs of its owners.

Sometimes in families, a desire arises to run from your history. Yes, your family enterprise protects you. Yes, it offers you a certain amount of flexibility as the years pass. But if co-ownership exasperates you and trusts exhaust you, you may be tempted to think you can live your life apart from your history. You may want to cut ties, move to a different part of the world, and start from scratch. This thought, though sometimes appealing, overlooks an essential truth. You could be better off—physically, emotionally, intellectually, socially, spiritually, even financially—if you leave town. But your leaving will not eradicate the events that came before this moment. Every moment in the past has happened. Every moment in the future will happen. The continuum of moments, spread across the entirety of your life, comprises *your* ownership. Like it or not, your ownership is tied to your personal history.

The question remains, how will you take ownership of what you own? How will you activate your ownership as you make your way through time?

Our kitchen project moved quickly, and soon we were conferring with the contractor about electricity. We had all the typical discussions—where will the outlets go, how many switches will there be, what will the fixtures look like. We had decisions to make, and we were having trouble deciding.

The contractor looked us in the eye and said, patiently and directly, "Only you can flip the switch."

This contractor, himself a second-generation leader of a family business, encapsulated the truth about ownership. Only you can flip the switch. Only you can activate the ownership that belongs to you.

You may not be the sole owner. You may not be the majority owner. You may not be the legal owner. It's certain that you will not be the forever owner.

But right now, at this point in time, you *are* an owner—and to put your ownership to use, you must turn it on.

HOW CAN I DO WHAT IT TAKES?

To turn it on, you must do five things.

First, you must appreciate the setting and the history.

Your "house"—that is, your enterprise—was created at a point in time by a person. Maybe that person was you. Maybe that person lived generations before you. Maybe you had the advantage of knowing the person. Maybe you didn't. Whatever the case, there was a person who got the ball rolling. The ball did not roll due to some inhuman system, structure, or process. It started rolling due to action of a person. That person was not perfect. Neither are you. Nor will the owners who come after you be perfect.

Take my house, for example. Not every change to our house has been an improvement. Some of the carpentry from several owners ago is amateurish. The floorplan, where the additions intersect the old part, is still odd. Especially with the additions to the back of the house, guests still do not use the front door.

At my house, I do not claim to be an absolutely better owner than those who came before me. I'm not the apex of the past 100 years. Those who come after me may have great ideas for improvements that never crossed my mind. My wife and I, though, have made our own improvements, and we have corrected mistakes, our own and our predecessors'. Recall the Good Enough Standard from Chapter 3. We have made our house good enough—better than good enough, actually.

Second, you must learn the ownership structure.

You are unique. Your family is unique. As a result, the ownership structure of your enterprise—each of the enterprises—is unique. The structure is especially unique if a trust owns it. As we saw in Chapter 4, a person creates a trust to benefit someone else. The person who sets up the trust is unique, and the person being benefited is unique.

This means you must learn *your* ownership structure, and you must take it on its own terms. Comparing it to someone else's, and trying to appraise it in terms of "best practices," doesn't get the job done. Comparison will distract you, and "best practices" could mislead you. You must go farther than that. You must look at the ownership as it was intended to be. Most of all, you must understand its creators as they understood themselves. Only then will you be ready to know and do what needs to be done today.

Third, you must understand your Unique Ability and those of your co-owners.

Taking your enterprise on its own terms doesn't mean you abandon any thought of improving it. If you are serious about taking your own ownership of it, of course you will be thinking about how to make it better. You do this by looking to what is present, not what is absent. And you uncover what is present by tapping Unique Ability, your own and those of your co-owners.

When sizing up your Unique Ability, be sure to differentiate those activities where you experience energizing passion and those activities at which you are merely excellent. Yes, you want to stop performing any activities at which you are incompetent or mediocre. Once you stop them, though, a critical line arises between "excellent" and "Unique Ability." Aim to spend most of every week on the Unique Ability side of the line.

As the saying goes, "This is too good not to be better."

Fourth, you must look for opportunities to practice Entrepre-

neurial Stewardship.

As we discussed in Chapter 7, Entrepreneurial Stewardship is not a simple or easy way to go through life. It's not for everyone. Some families do not have anyone who is or could become an Entrepreneurial Steward. Still other families do not even have outside help to fill the role.

For those who do, looking for opportunities to practice Entrepreneurial Stewardship is essential. As an Entrepreneurial Steward, you have a solid handle on your own Unique Ability and those of your co-owners. You cultivate good habits, especially in the disciplined earning, saving, and spending of money. Most fundamentally, you cultivate a healthy relationship with ambition. You appreciate the difference between possessing things out of greed and owning things out of virtue.

Eventually, you'll be the one who chooses the next Entrepreneurial Steward in your family.

Fifth, you must come to terms with gratitude.

Gratitude is the ability to appreciate something good done for you. Ideally, it is also the ability to express your appreciation to the person who did the good for you.

Gratitude is essential to ownership. Ingratitude damages ownership, and gratitude deepens ownership.

The lack of gratitude obstructs a person's ability to be an effective owner. You won't be a true owner for long if all you do is consume. You can't be an effective beneficiary if you're angry at the person who created your trust. You can't be an effective member of an LLC if you spend your time seeking revenge on a fellow member. You cannot be a reasonably happy child if you constantly resent your parents. You cannot be a reasonably happy parent if you constantly complain about how your child has turned out.

The existence of gratitude, by contrast, sharpens your sense of how you affect what happens to what you own. Think back to Chapter 1, where the circles ripple out. You realize you alone do not create the ripples. You have help from the people who work with you. You have help from customers in every community where you do business. You have help from every family member who uses their non-financial capital.

With gratitude, you realize that with your Unique Ability, you exercise an influence that no other owner does—not any of your co-owners, not a trustee, not any other beneficiary, and not any of the owners who preceded you. You have a more accurate sense of perspective.

Gratitude also confers two other big advantages:

For assets owned in trust, gratitude helps you become a Self-Governing Beneficiary.

For all assets, in trust or not, gratitude enables you to be a fully Responsible Owner.

Taking action in these five ways will give you the confidence to resolve the Integrity Problem in your own life. You'll come to terms with your house, and you'll see the importance of you being an owner of it right now, at this particular point in time. *You* are an owner *now*.

Only you can take ownership of what you own.

Only you can activate the ownership that belongs to you.

Only you can flip the switch.

So do it—with confidence, with gratitude, and with the satisfaction of taking your place in a long line of owners that have helped shape the lives of future generations.

FURTHER READING

Angus, Patricia M., *The Trustee Primer: A Guide for Personal Trustees* (2016)

Aristotle, *Nicomachean Ethics*, translated by Terence Irwin (Hackett 1985)

Babcock, Warner King, "Family Banks: Using Corporate Entities and Trusts", Trusts & Estates, July 3, 2013

Babcock, Warner King, "How to Properly Structure and Govern a Family Bank," Trusts & Estates, April 12, 2013

Blue, Ron, *Splitting Heirs* (Northfield Publishing 2004)

Bradley, Omar N., *A General's Life* (Simon and Schuster 1983)

Brooks, Arthur C., *From Strength To Strength: Finding Success, Happiness, and Deep Purpose in the Second Half of Life* (Portfolio 2022)

Collier, Charles, *Wealth In Families*, 2d ed. (Harvard University 2008)

Diamond, Martin, "Ethics and Politics—The American Way," in *As Far As Republican Principles Will Admit: Essays by Martin Diamond* (AEI Press 1992)

Diamond, Martin, "The Federalist: 1787-1788," in *As Far As Republican Principles Will Admit: Essays by Martin Diamond*

Eliot, T.S., "Little Gidding," Four Quartets, in *The Complete Poems and Plays* (Harcourt, 1950)

Eliot, T.S., *Murder In The Cathedral*, in *The Complete Poems and Plays* (Harcourt, 1950)

Eliot, T.S., *The Family Reunion*, in *The Complete Poems and Plays* (Harcourt, 1950)

Emerson, Ralph Waldo, "Circles," Essay (1841); see https://emersoncentral.com/texts/essays-first-series/circles/

Erwin, Michael S., and Willys Devoll, *Leadership Is A Relationship: How to Put People First in the Digital World* (Wiley 2022)

Faulkner, Robert, *The Case For Greatness: Honorable Ambition and Its Critics* (Yale University Press 2007)

Goldstone, Hartley, and James E. Hughes, Jr. and Keith Whitaker, *Family Trusts: A Guide For Beneficiaries, Trustees, Trust Protectors, and Trust Creators* (Wiley 2016)

Grubman, James, and Dennis Jaffe and Kristin Keffeler, *Wealth 3.0: The Future of Family Wealth Advising* (Family Wealth Consulting 2023)

Haidt, Jonathan, *The Anxious Generation: How the Great Rewiring of Childhood Is Causing an Epidemic of Mental Illness* (Penguin Press 2024)

Hamilton, Alexander, and James Madison and John Jay, *The Federalist: A Collection of Essays Written in Favor of the New Constitution* (Center for Judicial Studies 1990)

Hughes, Jr., James E., *Family: The Compact Among Generations* (Bloomberg Press 2007)

Hughes, Jr., James E., and Susan E. Massenzio and Keith Whitaker, *Complete Family Wealth* (Wiley 2018)

Jensen, Steven J., *The Human Person: A Beginner's Thomistic Psychology* (Catholic University of America Press 2018)

Kethledge, Raymond M., and Michael S. Erwin, *Lead Yourself First: Inspiring Leadership Through Solitude* (Bloomsbury Publishing 2018)

Kreeft, Peter, *A Summa Of The Summa: The Essential Philosophical Passages of St. Thomas Aquinas' Summa Theologica Edited and Explained For Beginners* (Ignatius Press 1990)

Lafley, A.G., and Roger L. Martin, *Playing To Win: How Strategy Really Works* (Harvard Business Review Press 2013)

Lucas, Stuart, Wealth: *Grow It And Protect It*, revised edition (FT Press 2013)

Maclean, Norman, *A River Runs Through It And Other Stories*, 25th anniversary edition (University of Chicago Press 2001)

McCracken, Ken, *The Alternative Family Business Dictionary* (2022)

McCullough, David, *1776* (Simon and Schuster 2005)

Moulton, Gary, ed., *The Lewis and Clark Journals: An American Epic of Discovery, by Meriwether Lewis, William Clark, and the Corps of Discovery* (University of Nebraska Press

2003)

Nomura, Catherine, and Julia Waller and Shannon Waller, *Unique Ability 2.0: Discovery—Define Your Best Self* (The Strategic Coach, Inc. 2015)

Peppet, Scott, "Monitoring Financial Capital With the 'Four Horsemen' Graph," in *Wealth of Wisdom: Top Practices for Wealthy Families and Their Advisors*, chapters arranged by Tom Cullough and Keith Whitaker (Wiley 2022)

Plutarch, "Julius Caesar," *Lives of The Noble Grecians and Romans*, translated by John Dryden (Modern Library)

Plutarch, "Publius Valerius Publicola," *Lives of The Noble Grecians and Romans.*

Renkert-Thomas, Amelia, *Engaged Ownership: A Guide For Owners Of Family Businesses* (Wiley 2016)

Roosevelt, Theodore, "Citizenship In A Republic," speech (1910); see https://www.presidency.ucsb.edu/documents/address-the-sorbonne-paris-france-citizenship-republic

Roosevelt, Theodore, *Ranch Life and the Hunting Trail* (Dover Publications 2009)

Richards, Pierre, and Howard I. Gross, *The Trustee's Guide: A Handbook for Individual Trustees, Beneficiaries, and Advisors* (Tower Publishing 1999)

Scott, Austin Wakeman, and Mark L. Ascher, *Scott and Ascher On Trusts* (6th ed.) (Wolters Kluwer 2019)

Scott, Susan, *Fierce Conversations: Achieving Success At*

Work & In Life, One Conversation At A Time (Berkley 2017)

Sullivan, Dan, *Industry Transformers* (The Strategic Coach Inc. 2008)

Sullivan, Dan, *The Four C's Formula* (The Strategic Coach Inc. 2021)

Sullivan, Dan, *Your Attention: Your Property* (The Strategic Coach Inc. 2021)

Wilder, Thorton, *The Happy Journey To Trenton And Camden*, in *Collected Plays & Writings On Theater* (Library of America 2007)

Wilder, Thorton, *The Long Christmas Dinner*, in *Collected Plays & Writings On Theater* (Library of America 2007)

Willis, Thayer Cheatham, *Beyond Gold: True Wealth For Inheritors* (New Concord Press 2012)

Wojtyla, Karol, *The Jeweler's Shop*, Three-act play, translated by Boleslaw Taborski (Ignatius Press 1992)

THREE CIRCLE MODEL: BLANK WORKSHEET

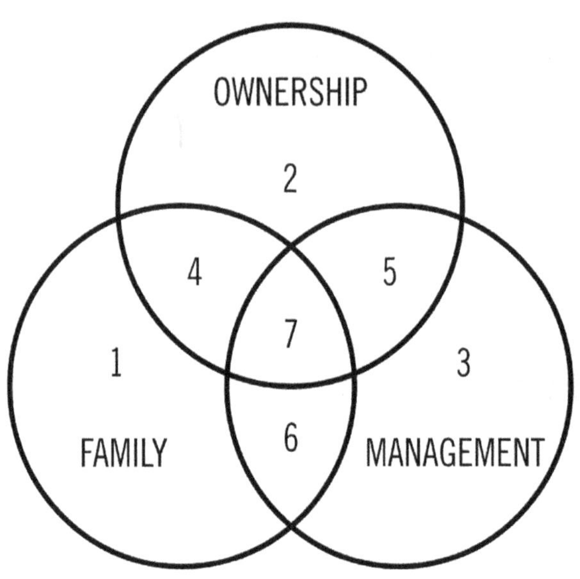

ACKNOWLEDGMENTS

I wish to thank the following people for their roles in helping bring about this book.

Meghan McCracken and her undaunted team of book experts at Brilliant Media. This book would not have happened without them. They are the best in the business.

My parents—my first teachers, my oldest friends, and trailblazers.

Jay Hughes of Aspen, Colorado—the preeminent thinker in the field.

Ken McCracken of Glasgow, Scotland, and Amelia Renkert-Thomas of Durham, North Carolina, for their far-sighted leadership in the field, their attention to process, and their thoroughgoing desire to help.

Dr. John and Jenny Warford of Bismarck, Burleigh County, North Dakota, who unknowingly gave me the idea to investigate the Lewis and Clark expedition.

My coaches at Strategic Coach—Colleen Bowler, Mary Miller, and Adrienne Duffy. Each of you has shaped my thinking in ways you will never know.

Stuart Lucas and the University of Chicago, a superior teacher at a superior school.

Dominican Fathers Kenneth R. Letoile, O.P., and John Langlois, O.P., for guidance about life.

My long-time business associate, LeeAnn Bareswilt, for her common sense, steadiness, and judgment.

My law and business partners in my various ventures, for putting the customer first.

All the authors of works cited in this book. They created vehicles to aid my understanding.

Last and most important, my wife, Chris, our four children and their spouses, and the grandchildren, who put up with me during the process of creating this book. I am pleased at what is happening in our family.

David W. Burleigh
Cincinnati, Ohio
June 2024

ABOUT THE AUTHOR

David W. Burleigh is a family ownership expert. An attorney by background, he deals with how families own things—trusts, LLCs, corporations, partnerships—and what they own—private operating companies, investment accounts, real estate, and all kinds of other property.

Over the course of his career, he has helped clients protect and develop over $1 billion in assets. He is also a fiduciary for clients who require unbiased, independent thinking with their trusts, and is the sole professional in the Midwest region to hold the Advanced Certificate in Family Enterprise Advising from the Society of Trust and Estate Practitioners.

David and his wife, Christin, live in a 100-year-old farmhouse near Cincinnati with their intrepid Norfolk terrier, Charlie.

www.ingramcontent.com/pod-product-compliance
Lightning Source LLC
Chambersburg PA
CBHW031401180326
41458CB00043B/6570/J

* 9 7 8 1 9 6 2 3 4 1 4 9 3 *